# CULTURE SHOCK!

## Norway

**Elizabeth Su-Dale**

·K·U·P·E·R·A·R·D·

**In the same series**

| | | |
|---|---|---|
| *Australia* | *Indonesia* | *Philippines* |
| *Britain* | *Israel* | *Singapore* |
| *Burma* | *Italy* | *South Africa* |
| *Canada* | *Japan* | *Spain* |
| *China* | *Korea* | *Sri Lanka* |
| *France* | *Malaysia* | *Taiwan* |
| *Hong Kong* | *Nepal* | *Thailand* |
| *India* | *Pakistan* | *USA* |

**Culture Shock! Norway**
First published in Great Britain by
Kuperard (London) Ltd
No 9, Hampstead West
224 Iverson Road
London NW6 2HL
1995

Illustrations by TRIGG
Cover photographs from APA Photo Agency ·
and The Image Bank
Photographs from Elizabeth Su-Dale
and Royal Norwegian Embassy, Singapore

Printed in Singapore

ISBN 1-85733-088-9

*To my family:*
*Ole, Lise, Sonja, Andreas, and Dag Dale;*
*and*
*to all the families and individuals in Leikanger*
*who made my stay in Norway a memorable one*

# CONTENTS

# PREFACE

Writing a book about the culture and people of a country as vast as Norway is a mountain of a challenge. When I was first invited to write *Culture Shock! Norway* a year ago, I responded with great enthusiasm and excitement. I wanted to share my experience of Norway with people who did not know much about this rich and beautiful land, and whose only idea of Norway was that it was way up north, too far north to be on the agenda of their tour itineraries, and too cold to visit.

Norway *is* a little further north than Copenhagen, the location of Scandinavia's international airport.

Norway's climate and terrain have left an indelible mark on the national character. Norwegians are basically simple, sincere people who love nature and the outdoors. Their coastal maritime industry has also meant exposure to other cultures. Norwegians are Europeans first and foremost, but at the same time, they are internationalists, very much aware of the currents of international politics and upheaval, and sensitive to the demands for environmental concern and control.

Norwegians strive to maintain, and ultimately to improve, their quality of life. Their search for a meaningful, harmonious, and peaceful coexistence with nature and each other has led to an unstated but manifest desire to struggle for, and achieve, a sense of equilibrium, both without and within.

The chapters in this book have been arranged to encourage the reader to tour through the mystique of Norway and its people. It cannot be a comprehensive account of Norwegian culture – no one book can give this. But if I have engaged you and aroused your curiosity to learn more about, and perhaps even to visit Norway or get to know Norwegians in your own local community, I would be happy. *Culture Shock! Norway* would then be less of a shock and more of a surprising discovery.

# Chapter One

# LAND OF FJORD AND MOUNTAIN

Norway is a land of contrasts: it is the country of fjord and mountain; a sprawling urban conurbation in the big cities and a vast landscape of tilled land. Norway is also the Land of the Midnight Sun. One-third of the land, the northernmost part of the country, stretches above the Arctic Circle and catches the sun for six months of the year, letting it go for another six months, when it suffers the deprivation of light.

Norway's long strip of coastline is marked by inward excursions into valleys and hills. Its 386,958 square kilometres of land is populated by 4.3 million people distributed over the hills and dales, living in solid, traditional homesteads handed down over generations,

*The graceful lines of mountain and sea unfold as you travel along the fjords. Norway fjords are the result of the melting of glaciers during the last Ice Age.*

in cosy little apartments in grey city blocks, or in charming wooden or brick houses dotting the mountainsides. Norway's size and relatively small population are distinctive characteristics for which its people sometimes feel they have to apologise.

Norway also comprises the islands of Svalbard (62,700 square kilometres) and Jan Mayen (380 square kilometres) northeast of the mainland.

Norway is still very Europe-centred in trade. Its primary trading partners are Britain, Sweden, Denmark, Germany, Japan, and the United States of America. Its primary exports are ships, offshore equipment, advanced machinery, petroleum, chemicals, fish and fish products, iron, steel and ferro-alloys, paper, and cardboard.

Up north, Norway is inhabited by the Sami people whose main

occupation is still reindeer rearing. When the Chernobyl disaster struck in the Soviet Union in 1986, the Sami settlers suffered great losses since thousands of reindeer were affected by the contamination of their pastureland, which had received the radioactive fallout from Chernobyl in the form of rain and particles. This incident highlights the vulnerability of Norway to influences from its neighbours in Europe. It cannot afford to live in solitude.

The issue of joining the European Community in the 1970s and 1990s provoked considerable debate. Independence and full autonomy came late to this European country. Although Norway is an old kingdom, it was in a union for about 400 years with Denmark, and thereafter with Sweden. It was only in 1905 that Norway reestablished its independent status as a self-governing country, throwing off the shackles of Swedish domination.

Norway is probably also one of the most democratic and classless societies in the world. Democracy is not just a catchword but is a deep-rooted philosophy. Norwegians take an active interest in political life – from the local municipal level to the national level. Hence the notions of independence and self-governance are fiercely protected. Autonomy is too newly-earned and too valuable to be traded for illusory dreams of European union, which would again mean subservience in an interactive form. The Norwegians have to think about that before they commit themselves to joining the European Community.

And this is yet another national trait. Norwegians like to think and debate things through. They are like Rodin's thinker, poised in his attitude of deep reflection and unwavering concentration. They need to discuss and have a consensus before the country plunges into this chasm of mutual self-help interlinkage.

Norwegians are hardworking. Long before the North Sea oil wells gave additional prosperity, Norway had, through hard work, become one of the wealthiest nations in the world. Its wealth, more than anywhere else in the world, is based on the egalitarian principle.

## *CLIMATE*

Normally, the closer you get to the polar regions, the more barren and desolate the natural environment becomes. A pleasant surprise awaits you in Norway.

The warm waters of the Gulf Stream could not have been more fortuitous for the Norwegian coast. Fjord Norway in particular therefore enjoys a temperate and mild climate all year round. If you take the coastal express service you will, once you have rounded North Cape towards Kirkenes, be further north than both Siberia and the continent of North America. In spite of this you will find green forests, and on fine days people sunbathing on the chalk-white beaches along the coast.

Average temperatures for Oslo and Bergen range from about 0°C in winter to about 16°C in July. In Vardø, the northernmost town, the average winter temperature is about –5°C as against 10°C in July. The temperature in northern Norway can also reach as high as 25–30°C during the summer.

Naturally, the north is also cool during summer, but it does have the Midnight Sun, ensuring 24 hours of daylight. It is an amazing experience to have a drink at midnight in full daylight and watch the sun hovering over the horizon. The winter days, however, can be long, and longer the further north you get. Most people coming north from southern Norway therefore have problems in adjusting themselves to the lack of sunshine during the winter months.

## *ECONOMY*

For generations Norwegians earned their living from nature. They had to learn the importance of living in harmony with nature. Environmental protection therefore became a practical reality long before it became an international issue. Nature is not confined to nature reserves and national parks. You will find it never leaves you wherever you travel in Norway.

Nature has dictated the terms, and laid the foundations for the development of modern Norway. Selected waterfalls and rapids have been tamed to provide electricity. Roads pass through tunnels blasted through or cut across the high mountains. Some of the world's longest bridges link hundreds of islands to the mainland. Every day the most advanced technology pumps thousands of barrels of oil from the North Sea.

Norwegians have one of the highest per capita incomes in the world. North Sea oil and gas fields are one of the cornerstones of the economy. Other major industries are fishing, pulp and paper, wood, mining, manufacturing, and shipping.

Norway has a mixed economy of state-owned and privately owned corporations. Public utilities are state-owned, but the trend is towards privatisation. Over the last few decades employment in agriculture, forestry, and fisheries has declined rapidly, while there has been a notable increase in manufacturing and services, and education and health services. Exports account for about 50% of the total Gross Domestic Product.

More than half the work force is employed in commerce, transport and communications, administration, and other services; one-third in manufacturing, mining, building and construction, power and water supply; and less than one-tenth in agriculture, forestry and fishing.

## MAJOR CITIES

The three largest cities are Oslo, the capital that is home to about 500,000 people, Bergen (about 200,000), and Trondheim (about 140,000). Approximately 70% of Norwegians live in towns and urban communities. But the Norwegian notion of town and city is rather different from the dense, concentrated conurbations of metropolises such as New York. In Norway, the city is sprawling; it spreads itself out because of the country's topography. First-time visitors from other countries look at Oslo and wonder why the streets are not always packed with people and few skyscrapers graze the sky; what they do not know is that this is the result of a deliberate planning policy.

Oslo, the capital of Norway, is situated in the southern part of the country at the head of the Oslofjord. The city is the gateway to Norway and the main centre for communications, trade, education, research, industry, and transport. It is also a major centre for international shipping. Norway's political and financial leaders are based in Oslo. While the city has a population of 500,000, the Oslo region, Norway's largest urban area, has 900,000 inhabitants.

Stavanger, the oil capital of Norway, is located on the southwestern coast where the landscape changes from high mountains to fertile valleys and a coastline dotted with hundreds of islands. Apart from the petroleum-related development, research, and training facilities, Stavanger is also home to extensive research and production in the fields of agriculture, farm machinery, fish farming and processing, medicine, and hotel administration.

Bergen, called the Capital of the Fjords, is situated on the west coast of Norway. It is the ideal departure point for excursions to the fjord areas. Although its population is only about 200,000, it has the facilities of a major city, including good theatres and concert halls. The Bergen Festival held every year in May is worth visiting. Bergen grew as a trading centre, servicing the coastal regions and with external links to Germany and England. It is today also a major industrial centre. The University of Bergen has well developed research facilities focusing on subsea technology, medicine, high tech sectors, and business administration.

Trondheim, Norway's third largest city and the centre of Mid-Norway, is the country's ancient capital. The city will celebrate its thousandth anniversary in 1997. Today, Trondheim is Norway's centre for technological education and research. The university and the Norwegian Institution of Technology also provide opportunities for maritime, technical, and medical research.

Tromsø, which lies far north of the Arctic Circle, has majestic natural surroundings between the sea and mountains towering up to 2000 metres. It is the world's northernmost university city and

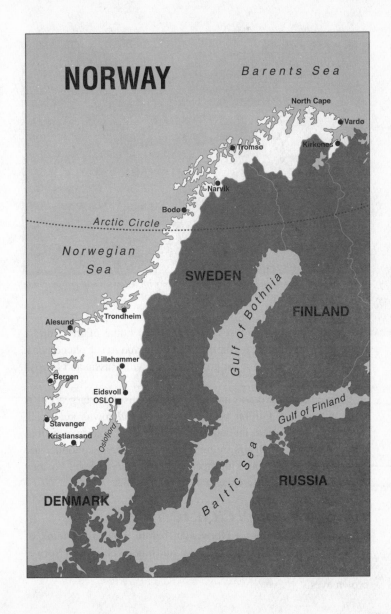

*A picturesque little town in the Lofoten islands, with its own sheltered quayside for hobby craft. Lofoten is famous for its fish products.*

Northern Norway's largest centre. It is the home of the world's leading research centre for the northern lights and Arctic phenomena. The city is the centre for the growing trade with Russia and for fish processing and export.

As mentioned, Norway has no big metropolises: the largest city is Oslo with half a million people. Its cities and towns are small. However, they possess an unusually high level of quality as well as public participation in arts, culture, and sports. Their economic base is a reflection of Norway's high technology and service level, but they also offer regional differences and specialisations.

## THE NORWEGIAN CHARACTER

If you have never met a Norwegian before, you might think of someone blonde and Nordic, tall, lean, and blue-eyed. Not all Norwegians are tall and blonde; some are short, brown-haired, and have brown eyes.

Going beyond physical appearance, you can recognise a few distinguishing characteristics as being asymmetrically Norwegian. Running the risk of stereotyping a nation's people, it is easy to categorise Norwegians into types identifiable by certain traits.

## *The Simple Norwegian*

Norwegians like to believe they are simple people with simple tastes, easy to please, and with principles and values they uphold with honesty and sincerity. There are many Norwegians like that. They are not ostentatious. They eat simple meals – just give them milk, bread, cheese, potatoes, and a hot roast. Nothing too fancy. They would not mind French cordon bleu once in a while, but might take time to learn French tastes.

Yet they are very well educated. The educational level of Norwegians is among the highest in the world. You will find that they are well read in what is happening in faraway places. At home, they collect works by local artists, mainly lithographs or oils. They dress in sweaters in winter, sensible clothes in summer. Sports and outdoor life play a very important part in their daily routine. In the winter, they like to go skiing. During summer, there is extensive participation in soccer, athletics, swimming, and a wide range of other outdoor sports.

The Simple Norwegian is not impressed easily by names and titles. Don't think you can show how important you are by mentioning that you know some minister or their superior. Norway is an egalitarian society and relationships are based on democratic principles of respect and familiarity. The Simple Norwegian will like you for yourself and respect you for what you are, not for whom you know. Don't show off your artistic sensibilities by rattling off the names of prominent artists. There is undoubtedly a certain degree of parochialism concerning cultural matters. As mentioned earlier, Norway can be an insular society.

Simple Norwegians are people of the soil. They like to potter around in the garden in the summer, working to make it a place of green and shade. Stones and rocks have to be cleared, soil put in place, trees planted and weeds pulled. It is hard work preparing the land to be a garden at times. But the Simple Norwegian relishes the task and sees it as a pleasurable duty.

Simple Norwegians also like to go for walks in the forests or in the mountains. They bring their dog out for a run in the evenings. If they enjoy skiing, they will do practice runs on the road in summer – skating along on skis on rollers on the hard road, using ski sticks to propel them along in a simulation of a cross-country ski.

## The Nature Rambler

Norwegian Nature Ramblers are another common breed. They enthuse about the pleasures of nature. *Å gå på tur* (to go for walks) is their byline. They love to be out in the mountains amid the lingonberries and blueberries in the autumn. When it is early spring, they take solitary walks and see the remnants of snow and the disappearing traces of ski trails marked out in the grasses. Their nature is solitary, gentle, and attuned to the sky and the trees.

If you visit the home of Edvard Grieg in Bergen, you will understand how Grieg composed his famous *Peer Gynt* suite. His music study is housed separately in a little cottage on a rock jutting out into the sea. The table at which he composed overlooks a panoramic view of the sea with the towering mountains seen in a haze of romantic allusion. Paths cut through the surrounding forest. The environment is rustic and soothing to a person who likes to live and create amidst the verdant green of nature and the rugged majesty of mountain and sea. You could almost imagine Grieg taking walks along the forest paths, looking out to sea, imagining and hearing the mysterious magic of the trolls in the mountains and picturing the shadowed landscape of mourning figures up a hill in the dignified rhythm of 'Åse's Death'. (Åse, Peer Gynt's mother, is an ardent supporter and a believer of his self-created myth.)

Norwegians like to go for nature rambles because they afford

*Two Norwegians, a mother and her daughter, in their beautifully embroidered* bunad *or national costume, complete with silver earrings, brooch, and belt.*

glimpses of peace and sanity. *Å få fred og ro* is a common expression which means 'to find peace and calm'. Indeed, a Norwegian can be characterised by this desire to find peace 'under the elms', so to speak.

Many Norwegians also have vacation houses or *hytter*, which are their places of retreat. About one-third of Norwegians own a second home in the mountains or at the seaside. If you are invited to one, then you are part of the family.

## *The Lover of Peace*

Norwegians are typically lovers of peace. They believe in the virtue of human rights and will fight to uphold justice and equality. They are idealists, and because of their creditable ideals, they may exhibit a certain degree of political naiveté, compared with the political savvy of their European comrades. Norwegians not only speak words of

19

peace, they believe in words of peace. They accept another's words as words of honour until they find out that not all humans are honourable.

Norwegians tend to believe that all humans should live in peace and harmony. Indeed, living in the splendour of fjord and mountain in Norway almost convinces you that there is indeed peace on this earth, and it is in Norway. Depending on where you reside in Norway, after a number of years there, you may begin to feel cut off from the rest of the contentious world. The relative stability of Norwegian politics, the enduring rhythm of the seasons, and the pattern of life lull you into a sense of well-being and satisfaction. But if you are energetic and must have change, the steady rhythm may bring impatience and frustration.

Norwegian Lovers of Peace hail all environmental efforts to protect nature and wildlife. They also celebrate the vindication of peace in conflict-ridden societies and accept refugees of persecution from other countries in an embrace of humanitarian compassion. Norway has accepted refugees from India, Pakistan, South America, Vietnam, and Africa. There have been some problems with assimilation of the refugees and acceptance by some Norwegian communities, but on the whole the response to political asylum has been very positive. However, most Norwegians do admit that while it is fine to say all should be free, to find a stranger on your doorstep, saying, 'Hi! I've come to live with you,' is a different matter altogether. This is especially so when some of the new arrivals have come for economic reasons rather than because of political persecution in their homeland.

## *The Internationalist*

Norway and Norwegians play an active role in international organisations. The United Nations' first Secretary-General was Trygve Lie, the representative from Norway. The first High Commissioner for Refugees under the forerunner to the United Nations – the League of Nations – was Fridtjof Nansen (a humanitarian and world-famous explorer). It was also Norway which arranged the secret talks between Israel and the Palestine Liberation Organisation, which finally led to a peace settlement after decades of war.

## The Concerned Environmentalist

The modern Norwegian is very much an environmentalist, engaged in the desire to safeguard nature and the environment. Among some Norwegians and Europeans, there is the perception that Norway is Europe's last wilderness. Only 3–4% of the country is built-up or arable land. Northern Europe's largest population of wild reindeer still wander across the endless expanses of untouched mountain plateaux. Wolverines and bears can still lead a relatively undisturbed life in wildlife mountain reserves.

In 1983, the United Nations established the World Commission on Environment and Development, headed by Norway's first woman prime minister, Gro Harlem Brundtland. In April 1987, this Commission presented its report, *Our Common Future*, which exhorted the world community and individual nations to pursue economic policies that did not place added stress on the environment, but instead strengthened and protected nature and resources. Norway took the World Commission's challenge seriously, and on 28 April 1989, the Brundtland government presented a comprehensive environment act to the Storting (Norwegian Parliament). The Norwegian environmentalist's motto is 'think globally, act locally'.

### Inky, the Octopus

Norwegian children and their parents all know and love a little blue octopus called Inky, the symbol of an environmental commitment that is unique in an international context. Inky's creator is Norwegian writer Bente Roestad, who, when a child, saw an octopus for the first time while on holiday in Greece. The memory of the little octopus returned to her when she began telling her 5-year-old nephew stories about life in the sea. Thus, the character of Inky was born.

Roestad's stories were published in a series of books about the wise little octopus and his friends who were concerned about pollution and the threat it posed to life in the sea. A television series grew out of this popularity, and when it was broadcast in conjunction with a call-in radio show, the response was tremendous. The switchboard was overwhelmed by a storm of telephone calls unprecedented in the history of the Norwegian Broadcasting Corporation (NRK). Over 40,000 children called the broadcasting company to say they were worried about pollution and wanted to do something to help save the environment. They wanted to know what they could do.

The Norwegian Society for Conservation of Nature, one of the country's leading environmental organisations, took up the challenge. It started the Inky Club for young environmental detectives. Today, the Inky Club has become the fastest growing environmental organisation in Norway, numbering about 17,000 members aged 5 to 13 in just a few years. Children have begun investigating environmental conditions in their neighbourhoods, writing articles for newspapers, and contacting politicians and industrial plants to urge them to take responsibility for the natural surroundings. Issues of particular concern to young sleuths include waste disposal, motor vehicle emissions, and wasteful packaging.

The Inky Club is a successfully growing organisation, thanks largely to the publicity environmental issues generates in the media and public consciousness, and to the quality of engagement and interactive commitment it engenders among its members. Your child can join the Inky Club too – all you have to do is write to the club at the address listed in an Inky book. Check it out with a librarian at the nearest public library.

## *The Champion of Human Rights*

The Norwegian is a defender of human rights. Norway gives the largest amount of development aid per capita of all the industrialised countries. It has been an important goal of Norwegian development cooperation policies that funding should benefit the poorest people. Countries that have benefited from Norwegian funding include China, Nepal, Pakistan, Bangladesh, India, Sri Lanka, Sudan, Ethiopia, Tanzania, Zambia, Mozambique, Botswana, and Zimbabwe.

Norway champions respect for human dignity and the protection of private individual values. There is an ombudsman, or government official, for consumer protection, an ombudsman for children, and an ombudsman for equality and civil rights. Certainly, human rights are given due recognition and Norwegians accord the greatest attention to treating everyone fairly.

## The Protester

There were already in the 1970s signs in the youth culture that Norwegian society was changing. Parts of the new age groups no longer proceeded into established frames.

The 1970s was the decade of leftwing movements. There were causes to demonstrate for. Albania and Mao's China became symbols of third world countries that did the right things. American involvement in the Vietnam War became a rallying point against imperialist exploitation everywhere. Other causes were nuclear power and pollution of the environment.

The 1980s' and 1990s' extreme protester is perhaps best represented by the punks. Their uniform consists usually of a pair of jeans (preferably with big holes), a large cardigan, and an 'Arafat' scarf, complemented by short hair and a nail or two either clipped into their faces or onto their clothing. The punks stand against the police and the welfare state – upon which they depend for their existence. Their attitudes seem to be characterised by a cynical resignation from life, which is also reflected in their make-up and clothes.

The punks are clearly different from previously described Norwegian 'types' in that they are a big city – in particular Oslo – phenomenon. They follow certain international trends, and they constitute a very small group of youths.

The protester of the 1970s had causes to demonstrate for, and the centres of activity were in colleges and universities. The early protesters have now graduated to become leaders in the established political and business communities. There are no longer any major causes, since yesterday's have largely disappeared. The modern punk movement is international in the way protest is expressed and is really about some young people losing faith in themselves and thus the ability to contribute to their society.

## *The DIY Norwegian*

Norway is very much a do-it-yourself society. There is nothing a male Norwegian in the countryside likes better than to build his new wall or renovate the cellar into a second sitting room. Some urban Norwegians will go home to their parents' place to hoe the grass on the farm, or do a painting job on their summer cabin. (Many Norwegians own summer homes near the sea or up in the mountains.)

The DIY man likes to work with his hands. Some Norwegians will even rent a cement-mixer to churn their own cement for the garden wall they are building. Other Norwegians like to paint or wallpaper their bedrooms or restore their grandmothers' antique chests of drawers to their former glory. What seems like hard work to most people is pleasurable expenditure of energy to a Norwegian.

After some time in Norway, you will also learn to be self-sufficient to a greater degree than when you lived in your home country. There are no maids in Norway so all the housework has to be done by the occupiers of the house. Meals have to be cooked. Gardens have to be weeded, and if it is a new home with a new garden, the soil has to be prepared for the growing of a garden. Norwegians transform little tasks like fixing the roof into projects and hobbies. They usually do not shirk responsibilities but relish the chance to be able to prove themselves capable and economical – in the sense they do not have to pay someone else to do it.

## The Modern Viking –
## Shipbuilder and Maritime Traditionalist

In the early history of Norway and Europe, the Viking raids were known to be quick, sudden, and relatively successful. The Vikings enjoyed their tactical superiority partly because of the efficiency of Scandinavian shipbuilding. A renowned Swedish archaeologist has written that the Viking ships are the only seaworthy amphibious landing vessels ever to be used in invasion forces. This explains some of the Vikings' military superiority.

Today, shipbuilding still accounts for a large part of Norwegian superiority and excellence. It is a well-known fact that the Norwegians are good shipbuilders. From 1850 to 1880, the merchant fleet increased substantially. During this period, Norway rose to third position among shipping nations. In the interwar period, it acquired a modern fleet of tankers.

As a result of high costs in the early 1980s, many shipowners registered their ships abroad. This led to a drastic drop in revenue from shipping and an alarming decrease in the number of Norwegian seamen. To revitalise Norwegian shipping, the Storting passed the Norwegian International Ship Register (NIS) Act in 1987. Through this register, shipowners could enter into local wage agreements with foreign seamen, thereby saving considerable fees in crew costs. In 1990, Norway's merchant fleet was once again the third largest in the world, and Norway had become an international centre for ship-broking and maritime insurance.

Being a seaman in the merchant navy in Norway is a good profession. Sailing the seven seas on a Norwegian ship is one way of seeing the world, and Norwegian seamen enjoy a respectable status. Norwegian Seamen Missions or Churches have been set up in various cities in the world to combine the missionary role of the Church and administer to the needs of seamen in port. Sometimes, these missions are a foreigner's first acquaintance with Norwegian culture.

## Norse Mythology

The Viking Age was an age of heathenism. A pantheon of gods and goddesses ruled over the earth. Odin, old and wise, was chief over them all. Tor (also known as Thor) was the god of the warriors and had a magic hammer called Mjalmar which, when hit against any other substance, produced a mighty roar of thunderous impact. The goddess Freya was responsible for the fertility of the soil and livestock. Loki was a trickster and a sorcerer, unreliable and distrusted by the other gods. The gods also had other dangerous adversaries – the *jotuns* – representing the darker side of life.

The Norse gods had human traits and, like their Greek counterparts on Olympus, they lived a bawdy, heathen life. They fought, ate, drank, fought ... Mortals who fell in battle went straight to Valhalla, the hall of the dead warriors, to join the gods in feasting.

In fact, the early Vikings lived in a violent society. Nearly all the Viking graves of males yielded weapons during excavation. A well-equipped warrior had a sword, a wooden shield with an iron boss at its centre to protect the hand, a spear, an axe, and a bow with up to 24 arrows. Yet even the graves with the most impressive array of weapons yielded signs of peaceful activities: sickles, scythes, and hoes lie buried alongside weapons.

Today, many male Norwegians bear the name Tor. Farm names such as Torshov, Froyshov, and Onsaker have kept their original heathen god-names. Present-day Norwegian place names with the last syllable *hov* indicate that there once was a heathen temple there.

## THE SAMI PEOPLE

The Winter Olympics in Lillehammer were opened by 40 reindeer rushing into the stadium drawing the traditional sleds devised by the Sami some 2000 years ago. Winter, snow, skis, reindeer – they are the Sami elements. Their participation at Lillehammer mark the acceptance of their cultural importance in Norwegian society.

The Sami people or Lapps, as they have been called, is a small, indigenous minority scattered throughout the northern parts of the Scandinavian countries and Russia. Half the world's Sami population of approximately 70,000 live in Norway. For centuries, the Sami have lived in close harmony with nature, following the reindeer herds on their annual migration. Their language and their traditional culture is distinctly different from those of the rest of Norway. They speak a Finno-Ugric language.

Their means of livelihood has included reindeer husbandry, farming, and fishing. But now, all this is changing. The lifestyle of the Sami has become much more like that in mainstream Norway. Most of them have exchanged the traditional lifestyle for a job in tourism or some other service, or in government administration.

The uniqueness of the Sami people is now fully recognised in comprehensive social and economic legislative acts, which include the establishment of a Sami Parliament in 1989 to which the Norwegian Parliament delegated specific areas of responsibility. A cultural revival is taking place, supported by public funding.

## *STATUTORY HOLIDAYS IN NORWAY*

Norwegians enjoy a total of 12 public holidays:

| | |
|---|---|
| New Year's Day | 1 January |
| Maundy Thursday | March/April |
| Good Friday | March/April |
| Easter Sunday | March/April |
| Easter Monday | March/April |
| Labour Day | 1 May |
| Ascension Day | April/May |
| Constitution Day | 17 May |
| Whit Sunday | April/May |
| Whit Monday | April/May |
| Christmas Day | 25 December |
| Boxing Day | 26 December |

## FESTIVALS AND RITES OF PASSAGE

Norwegians celebrate many occasions, some of which are specific rites of passage, such as *russ* (the Norwegian teenager's coming of age) and confirmation (a youth's acknowledgement of a Christian legacy and commitment to a faith many Norwegians embrace but fewer practise). A festival related to climatic change is the Midsummer Night bonfire, which celebrates the longest day in summer and the prelude to autumn and winter. Thanksgiving Mass in church gives thanks for autumn's bountiful harvest. Religious festivals include Christmas and Easter.

Many festivities are associated with religious rituals, but some have moved into the secular realm. These days are celebrated by all in Norway. Their significance might be different for different people, but the form of celebration is often the same.

### May 17 – Norway's National Day

Norway's national day, which falls on May 17, is the anniversary of the day the Norwegian constitution was first laid down in 1814 at Eidsvoll. Norway had declared itself independent from the union with Denmark but was later, in the same year, forced to accept a union with Sweden. The Norwegian Constitution, however, remained in force during the union, which lasted until 1905.

17th of May (*Syttende Mai*) was first celebrated in the 1840s. The poet, Henrik Wergeland, led a national romantic movement and was a pivotal force in making the 17th of May a day of national celebration. This national day was a children's day, and so it has remained.

On this day every Norwegian demonstrates a nationalistic pride in being Norwegian. The day begins with a big parade with numerous musical bands. People come bedecked in their finery, many (including little children) in their *bunad* or national costumes. (This is a luxury as the *bunad* is an expensive item of clothing, and children soon outgrow them. Norwegians usually wait till their children's confirmation day before getting the *bunad*.)

*Constitution Day on May 17 is also celebrated as Children's Day – with school bands, flags, and parades.*

May 17 is special because it is a day devoted to children. It is not celebrated in pomp and high style, with military displays of power and might. There are no tanks, no soldiers in uniform, no fighter jets zooming across the skies in daredevil stunts. There are no great and long speeches exhorting citizens to work harder for the future of the country, no political rallies. There are only people – masses of ordinary people including children. Indeed, May 17 could be mistaken for Children's Day as the children are honoured on that day by teachers and parents who prepare a funfair for them at the school grounds. There are games and sports events, magic shows and music, and the children have a good time. Parents and teachers man the stalls and sell food and drinks. Companies donate gifts for the lucky draws and as prizes. Every child goes home with some gift on May 17.

Lunch can be smoked salmon with omelette, or cured ham or cheese. The celebrations continue into the evening and the merry-makers sing and talk through the night.

## *May 1 – Labour Day*

In Norway, workers are remembered on May 1. Labour Day is marked in Norway with a parade by the trade unions and other interested parties. There are bands, banners, and processions. Local leaders and politicians may make speeches at public gatherings.

## *Easter Holiday* – **Påske**

Besides being a religious celebration, Easter is a big holiday in Norway because everyone gets a very long weekend when they can go up to the mountains to ski and acquire an Easter tan.

Norwegians go up to the mountains during Easter to enjoy nature and to tan themselves. The sun can be strong up in the mountains. Direct exposure to sunlight and light reflected off the snow can make one extremely tanned. A good tan is the pride of some Norwegian yuppies, who belong to the young and fashionable crowd. Families usually drive up to the mountains to spend the weekend in their mountain cabins.

Easter is also the time to eat *fastelavnsboller*, white buns with a rich cream and jam filling, dusted with icing sugar on top. They are a favourite with children, who usually get to do the filling and the top.

## *Advent*

Advent is a special time. Children make little clove balls – oranges with whole cloves stuck into the rind – and hang them by the window or place them in the kitchen. Their special fragrance reminds people that Christmas is coming.

Children who get Advent calendars mark off the days before Christmas. Advent calendars start with the first day of December, and as children tear off the passing dates they are rewarded with little chocolates hidden beneath the paper. Some mothers take the trouble to sew Advent calendars with little pockets for each day of December. They fill the pockets with treats like raisins or candy so their children will have little surprises to build up their anticipation of Christmas.

Outside, the landscape may be white and dark, but inside the home, there is warmth and laughter. The family usually lights an Advent candle for each week of Advent. The candles may be set in a series of four candles in a row. The first candle is lit on the first day of Advent and every evening of that first week. The second week of Advent will see another candle lit, the third week a third candle, until finally, by the fourth week, all four candles are aglow and a pretty sight on the table. Sometimes the candles are placed on the window sill, but in that case, they are usually electric candles, to avoid the risk of curtains catching fire.

Advent is the time when Norwegians hang up a star at their windows. It might be tinsel or wooden, or have an electric light bulb in it so it shines all night long. The star represents the Star of Bethlehem normally placed at the top of the Christmas tree.

## *Santa Lucia Celebrations*

Children celebrate the feast of Santa Lucia on 13 December when they commemorate the death of a young saint in Roman times who persevered in the face of adversity and adhered to her Christian faith. Primary school children dress in white and carry candles to signify the light of faith in the winter darkness. The boys wear conical hats and the girls wear silver tinsel in their hair. Parents are invited to an evening of song and food in the school hall and the children sing their special *Santa Lucia* song. Santa Lucia is a prelude to Christmas.

## *Christmas* – **Jul**

Christmas is celebrated by every Norwegian, Christian or otherwise. Apart from its religious connotations, it is a time of remembrance of loved ones and a re-affirmation of family ties.

Christmas is celebrated at school by teachers, parents, and children who dance around the big Christmas tree in the school hall and sing songs of joy and fun. Children eat waffles and raisin buns and drink juice. Parents see them perform in Christmas pageants and work

31

beside them to create little gifts and handicrafts. Family togetherness is emphasised and the message of forgiveness and love is prevalent.

There is always a Christmas tree. Norway has enough pines to make sure the Christmas tree tradition stays alive. Fathers buy a tree at the supermarket or order it from farmers who have pine forests.

Do not order your tree too late. One newcomer to Norway asked a colleague to get him a tree from his farm across the fjord. He made his request just a week before Christmas. The nights were getting dark very early and the colleague had to cross the fjord by boat to get home every evening. After four days, empty-handed and exasperated, he exclaimed, 'I tried. But every time I got home, it was so dark I could not see the trees in my forest!'

Christmas is a season of good food and beer or *aquavit*. Norwegians have Christmas dinners with specially smoked *pinneribbe* (mutton ribs), *lutefisk* (a fish delicacy), or a good roast of reindeer meat. Christmas is also the time for *gløgg*, a delicious concoction of juice with cloves, ginger, cinnamon, and raisins. Warm *gløgg* is guaranteed to make you a fan. There is always plenty to eat and you may be invited to dinner with your Norwegian friends, who are considerate of strangers in their midst.

Christmas is a time of giving. In Norway, it is the tradition that on Christmas Eve, presents are opened under the Christmas tree. Do not be late with your gifts because the fun lies in the anticipation.

Norwegian parents who observe tradition tell their children to leave a saucer of milk or a bowl of porridge for the *julenisse* or Christmas elf. This tradition originated in the farming community when this gesture acknowledged the blessings of the little farm elf who brought luck and good fortune to the farmer and his family.

Christmas is usually a time for family. It is also a time for parties. If you are a drinker, remember to make prior arrangements to be driven home by a friend or collected by a family member, or else you should order a taxi. Norway has strict driving laws and driving under the influence of alcohol means losing your licence straight away.

*Grilling sausages patiently over an open fire on Midsummer Night. It's a time for flower wreaths and fancy dress, and gaiety and song.*

## *Midsummer Night* – Jonsok

Midsummer Night, 23 June, is hailed as the most glorious night of summer. After this, autumn reigns and winter approaches. Hence, Midsummer Night or *Jonsok* is the night when everyone stays up late to witness the passing of the longest day in the year. It is a celebration to honour the sun, the light – and the longest day of the year.

*Jonsok* is celebrated by lighting a big bonfire in the neighbourhood. Everyone brings their unwanted wood, including old broken chairs, or collects dry branches to throw onto the bonfire pile. Children who have plaited crowns or wreaths of golden dandelions in their hair and boys who dress up as a Red Indian or cowboy watch in eager anticipation as the fire lights up the night sky. At 9 p.m., it is still light. Careful adults will spray the surrounding grass with water from a hose, just to make sure there is no fire hazard. There have been instances of grasses torching up because of an unusually dry summer. The hose is always nearby in case of an emergency.

Sausages make a hot sale as they are snapped up for barbecue parties around the bonfire. The nearby school field is transformed into a rally ground as friends and neighbours congregate for an evening of singing, dancing, eating, and laughing. *Jonsok* has a carnival atmosphere and some people put on fancy dress in keeping with the mood of gaiety and relaxed playfulness.

There is usually a procession in every neighbourhood precinct. It starts in the early evening with an accordionist, violinist, or other musician leading the way with a merry tune.

The accordion and violin play a special part in Norwegian merry-making. Their music is a hearty rendition of the song of Norway – plaintive echoes of lonely nights by the fireplace, cheerful jigs, melodious sighs in the night. Norwegians dance to the music of the violin or the accordion. Foreigners who are used to dancing only to canned disco music or the heavy rock rhythm of live disco bands may find it a little disconcerting at first to twirl to the music of a different wind. But once you get used to it, the music sounds beautiful and sometimes haunting. It provides good, sheer family fun as young dance with old and couples relive their romantic dancing days, and time flies.

## Russ

When Norwegians finish high school or upper secondary school, earlier called *gymnas*, they celebrate in style, going through a quite unusual ritual. The *gymnas* served the purpose of preparing its students to enter university. Graduates of the *gymnas* were known as *röd russer*, or the red russ, because they chose the colour red to grace their graduating 'gowns', which were really comfortable outfits resembling overalls. There is no real meaning to the term, but the significance and implications of being *russ* are many.

Graduating college students who are *russ* are identified by the special outfits they all choose to wear en masse. It can be red if they graduate from the school of arts, blue if they are from the economics

*A name card for a 'graduating' Russ student. Notice the little beret hanging jauntily at the edge of her picture. Her nickname reads "Den fråverande' (the reckless one). Below this title, she announces: 'All I want to do is illegal, immoral, or fattening'.*

colleges. *Russ* students also wear little matching berets of the same colour.

*Russ* celebrations last a few weeks after graduation. *Russ* students are allowed several liberties that they would not be allowed if they were not *russ*. One interesting phenomenon is that *russ* students are permitted to make a lot of noise. They can make noise almost anywhere and be tolerated because they are *russ*. They may be simply partying. They can also wake up their teachers early in the morning, sing songs at their teachers, put up posters and slogans, spray washable paint on pavements …

These acts of tolerable freedom are not acts of vandalism sanctioned by the rite of graduation. On the contrary, *russ* students are not allowed to destroy property – all they are permitted to do is have clean, noisy fun. And their elders recognise it as such. For example, if there is a stingy shopkeeper in the neighbourhood, *russ* students who feel strongly about him can put up a notice on his shop window, announcing 'Stingy Shopkeeper'. He might be embarrassed by it but he will accept it in the spirit of fun, and perhaps be less stingy in the future.

## *Baptism* – **Barnedåp**

Baptism is a ceremony that many Norwegians practise. It represents a significant rite of passage as it marks the child's entry into the Norwegian Church. Baptism involves family and close friends, and the selection and subsequent invitation of godparents. A baby usually has two sets of godparents, comprising two married couples. The godparents are supposed to be the moral guardians of the child and frequent contact is expected to be kept to ensure proper moral guidance and counselling.

The baby gets a special baptism gown, sometimes inherited from grandparents. The church service is then followed by lunch and little gifts for the baby (which could include the baby's first Bible). If there is a lunch party, neighbours are helpful and will volunteer to bake.

## *Confirmation* – **Konfirmasjon**

Most Norwegians are Lutherans. Even those who rebel against their Lutheran heritage and disavow themselves of any religious leanings will still encourage their children to go through with confirmation. Some young Norwegians may, however, decide to go through a *borgerlig* or 'civil' confirmation which, by its very name, is a contradiction, since confirmation is a religious ceremony as opposed to a secular one.

Confirmation is taken very seriously by adults and young people as it is a rite of passage. It represents the affirmation given by a young person of 14–15 years that he or she accepts a Christian birthright and agrees to abide by the principles of the Lutheran Church. The young person can now decide whether to remain a member of the Lutheran Church. Confirmation also celebrates a coming of age.

All aspiring confirmants go through a course lasting a couple of months to prepare them for their confirmation. They could come from the same class in the secondary school, go to the same church, and be instructed by the same pastor. Confirmation then becomes a very sociable activity.

The confirmation takes place in church. The group of aspirants are dressed in their Sunday best or their *bunad* (national dress). The *bunad* varies in richness and diversity, depending on the district the family comes from. Some *bunad* have embroidery; some are adorned with beadwork; others come in different colours.

When they enter the church, they have a gown of pristine white over their clothes. They say their vows and receive blessings. After the church service, which is attended by family and friends, each family gathers for a big family reunion celebration lunch, usually at the new confirmant's home or, if it is a really big party, at the church hall. This lunch is an important affair for Norwegians.

A confirmation party includes invitations to all relatives to join in the celebration. Normally, only relatives are invited as friends might be hosting their own parties, or there is just not enough space for friends. Relatives from out of town will make a special attempt to attend, so that a confirmation gathering is almost like a clan meeting. Aunts who were thought to have disappeared from the face of the earth suddenly reappear and cousins pop up from all over the place. It is quite a family do. Relatives are housed at neighbours' homes or even at the nearby ski lodges and hotels.

*Presents for the Confirmant*

Even if you were not invited to a confirmation party, it is much appreciated when you acknowledge this rite of passage your friend's daughter or son undergoes by giving a gift. You are also welcome to attend the church service in the morning. You can give your gift then or even before the confirmation itself. Silver is a good choice. Norwegians treat silver with the same respect the Chinese have for gold. Young female confirmants will be given silver buckles to adorn their *bunad*.

Silver earrings or brooches are popular gifts. If you have some pretty trinket or artistic handicraft from your own country, that makes a worthy gift as well. Norwegians are always appreciative of gestures, and a gift is always well received. You will find that there is a card in your mailbox a week later, with a picture of the new confirmant and a personal thank-you message for your kindness and your present. This is the Norwegian way of acknowledging your participation in this special ritual.

## SKIING IN NORWAY

There is a saying that Norwegians are born with skis on their feet. This merely highlights the importance of the sport in a Norwegian's life. In Norway, skiing was a natural consequence of the country's mountainous topography and heavy winter snows. Skis were a normal means of getting around in the winter, and skiing is the undisputed favourite among winter sports in the country. Norway has also pioneered the promotion of skiing as a sport for the disabled. Skiing has always been an important leisure pursuit for Norwegian children, doubtless because of its great potential for play and fun in the snow. Every year, thousands of children take part in Children's Day in Holmenkollen, the site of a great ski jump.

Modern skiing had its origin in the county of Telemark in the 19th century, but an ancient rock carving at Rodoy in Nordland county shows that Norwegians used skis as far back as 4,000 years ago. The oldest preserved ski excavated is a 2,300-year-old ski found in Finnmark in the far north. In Norwegian mythology, there is Ull, the god of skiing, and there is also Skade, the goddess of skiing and hunting. Serious interest in skiing first took root towards the end of the 19th century.

Growing interest in leisure activities led to the establishment of many ski clubs. The most popular type of skiing is still the cross-country ski trip. The combination of sport, exercise, and enjoyment of Norway's scenic landscape is a temptation many skiers cannot resist.

In 1952, Norway staged the Winter Olympics. In 1994, it played host yet again to the Winter Olympics at Lillehammer. This was a

*A skier along a main street in Lillehammer, site of the Winter Olympics of 1994.*

proud moment for Norway as it declared to the world its status as a nation that glorifies mass participation in sports as well as sports excellence and celebrates the physicality of life.

*The Telemark Ski*

The first skis made in the Middle Ages comprised a pair: one about 3 metres long and the other a shorter ski covered with animal skins,

39

with the hairs pointing backwards; this shorter ski allowed the skier to kick off more efficiently. These skis were abandoned around 1700 in favour of skis of the same length. But it was only in the 1860s that rapid development in ski equipment took place, largely because of the growing number of cross-country races. In this connection, the Telemark ski was the model.

In the 1870s and 1880s, Sondre Norheim of Telemark county in south Norway revived interest in skiing as a sport. Norheim, born in 1825, ended 4,000 years of tradition by using stiff ski bindings that enabled him to swing and jump without the risk of the skis falling off. He also designed a 'waisted' ski, the Telemark ski, the prototype of those now produced. Norheim was an unparalleled master of the art of skiing. He combined ordinary skiing with jumping and slalom and impressed his fellow countrymen in 1867 at the first national cross-country ski race held in Christiania (now Oslo).

To begin with, only one ski pole was used. But in 1887, cross-country skiers began using two poles. Around 1900, skiers started to wax the base of their skis in order to improve their sliding ability and grip on the snow. New types of bindings also made their appearance.

*The Slalom*
The word *slalom* originated in Morgedal, the home of Sondre Norheim. The first syllable, *sla*, means slope, hill, or smooth surface, while *låm* is the track down the slope. The normal *slalåm* or slalom was a cross-country run over fields, hills, and stone walls, weaving in and out among thickets. Today, the slalom is a competitor sport and has won enthusiasts in Europe and America.

*Norwegian Skis in America*
How did Norwegian skis get to America? For that is how the Americans learnt to get excited about skiing. The first Norwegian skis were brought to the United States by emigrants who crossed the Atlantic as early as 1825. A pioneer who kindled interest in skiing was

Jon Torsteinen Rui (Snowshoe Thompson) from Telemark (where else?), who maintained the only winter mail route over the Sierra Nevada from 1856 to 1876. Sondre Norheim was among those who promoted the sport of skiing in the United States when he emigrated in 1884.

## Norwegians in Chamonix

It would seem that skiing must be associated with Norway and no other country in Europe, for it was Norwegian students studying in France, Germany, and Switzerland who introduced the sport to their European counterparts at the end of the 19th century. Apparently, the Norwegian students saw the hillsides of Chamonix in France, where they were studying, and decided those hills were too good to waste, and so they hurtled down the slopes on their skis, sometimes using the roof of an old barn as an improvised ski jump.

Chamonix was then famous as a health centre or base for British mountaineers in the summer. Its hotels entertained guests in the summer and closed their doors at the onset of winter. When the Norwegians skied down the slopes of Chamonix, they demonstrated the potential for a new type of holiday and a new hotel season. It was also at their initiative that the first ski race in Germany was organised at Tauenberg, near Munich, in 1895. It did not come as a surprise when a Norwegian won the race.

Chamonix also gained international renown later when it hosted the first Winter Olympics in 1924. Norwegian skiers, led by Thorleif Haug, who was a legend in his time, took the first four places in the 50-kilometre race and 'showed the world the way'. Since that time, Norwegian skiers have won international acclaim in world-class ski competitions.

## The Birchlegs Race

A well-known skiing story in Norway is the story of the Birkebeiners (whose name means 'Birchlegs'), who became national heroes when they saved 2-year-old Prince Håkon Håkonsen from his pursuers in 1296. The Birchlegs were warriors and they got their name from their footwear, which consisted of animal skins wrapped around the legs and secured with birch roots. At that time, civil war was raging in Norway and the Birchlegs had to carry the young prince on their backs and flee over the mountains from Lillehammer, in the south of the Gudbrandsdal valley, to Rena in Osterdal, a valley further east.

The romance and heroism of the Birchleg warriors are immortalised in Lillehammer's coat-of-arms which bears an illustration of the Birchlegs' dramatic flight.

The Birchlegs' journey is commemorated every year in Norway when the Birkebeiner ski race, spanning 55 kilometres between Lillehammer and Rena, is held. More than 6,000 skiers compete in this race which is made more unusual by a burden the competitors have to carry on their backs, namely a 3.5 kilo backpack to represent the child who was brought to safety by the Birchlegs.

### Skiing at the Poles

Norway's pioneers in the world of sports have inspired many Norwegians to excel in outdoor sports, particularly skiing. Self-respect and pride in sporting achievements is high among Norwegians. Interest in skiing grew very quickly in Germany, France, Austria, and Switzerland after the great Norwegian explorer, Fridtjof Nansen, wrote of his love of skiing, which he regarded as the most typically Norwegian of all sports. In his book *The Crossing of Greenland*, which appeared in French, English, and German translations in 1890, Nansen declared that if anything deserved the name of the sport of sports, it had to be skiing. He had then just skied across Greenland's icecap from east to west in 1888.

Another intrepid Norwegian explorer is Roald Amundsen, who made a successful expedition with four other Norwegians to the South Pole in 1910–12. Amundsen planted the Norwegian flag at the South Pole in 1911, as the first man to reach this point. The five men covered a distance of about 3,000 kilometres on skis. Much of the equipment that Nansen and Amundsen used on their polar travels have been preserved for posterity and can now be viewed at the Ski Museum and the museum housing the polar ship *Fram* – both in Oslo.

Today, Norway is still inhabited by men with dreams and visions, modern Vikings who want to explore and conquer the world. Several Norwegian expeditions have followed in the ski tracks of the pioneers Nansen and Amundsen, both to the North and the South Poles. The most recent examples are Monica Kristensen and Erling Kagge.

To the overwhelmingly male-dominated ranks of explorers, it is refreshing to add the name of Monica Kristensen, who in 1986 led a South Pole expedition, following in the footsteps of Roald Amundsen. In 1989, she was awarded the prestigious Gold Medal of the Royal Geographical Society in London, becoming the first woman in 50 years to receive this award.

Erling Kagge, a 30-year-old Oslo lawyer, became in January 1993 the first man to go alone, and entirely unaided, to the South Pole. Kagge spent 50 days on the lonely, exhausting 1,310-kilometre journey from Berkner Island in the Weddell Sea to the Pole.

Although it means digressing a little, we should mention that the exploring spirit of Norwegians is also reflected in journeys into other waters. Thor Heyerdahl's expeditions are probably the most well known.

Heyerdahl launched a lifetime of daring deeds on the day after his wedding in 1937, when he voyaged with his bride to the Pacific in a bid to return to nature. Even then, he was concerned that mankind was destroying its environment through misuse and exploitation, a belief that made him a conservationist long before environmentalism became a popular cause.

His early experience in the Pacific provided the base for his theory that Polynesia could have been settled from Latin America rather than Asia as the anthropologists of the day contended. To prove this theory, he gathered a small group of Scandinavians with a similar urge for adventure, built a replica of the Peruvian log raft, named it *Kon-Tiki*, and set off on a 97-day voyage into international fame.

New expeditions and major scientific works followed – excavations on Easter Island with its strange statues, the Ra I and Ra II voyages across the Atlantic by reed boat, the Tigris voyage, and studies in the Maldive Islands and Peru.

Ragnar Thorseth is an example of the modern Viking spirit. His roots were in true Viking country – a small fishing village in the west coast region of Sunnmøre, home of hard-headed and determined individualists. Experienced seamen said it was madness when 20-year-old Thorseth announced his intention of rowing a 5 metre boat from the Norwegian west coast to the Shetland Islands in 1969. He completed the North Sea crossing, although with swollen fingers.

In the early 1980s, Thorseth launched a scheme to build a replica of a Viking *knarr* or ocean-going cargo ship. He named it *Saga Siglar* and sailed it in 1984 along the historic route of northern exploration from Norway to the Faeroes, Iceland, and Greenland. From the east coast of the USA and the Caribbean, the ship sailed back to Europe with a family crew, including his wife and sons. The *Saga Siglar* journeys have been followed by explorations with *Gaia*, a true copy of a Viking warship, demonstrating the exceptional seagoing capabilities of these ships.

## *Learn to Ski*

You will probably not wish to emulate these explorers, but when you live in Norway, it would be a pity if you did not try skiing. You might find you do not like it but an attempt should always be made. For people from countries that enjoy tropical climates and have no snow, skiing is a novelty. When you try to move about on skis, you feel like a duck that has got its feet wrong. And when you move down a modest slope in a poor imitation of a skier, you find your legs doing a gradual split so that you suddenly realise you were meant for acrobatics after all and not skiing!

Skis can be a little costly so you might not want to invest in a pair before you are sure you want to take up the sport. Do not be afraid to mention to your Norwegian neighbour that you do not have a pair of skis and are thinking of buying a secondhand pair or borrowing a pair for the day. You will find that your Norwegian neighbour is quite likely to come over to you with some pairs of secondhand children's skis that her children have outgrown. Just as Norwegians are generous with pass-me-down clothes (e.g. warm woollens for the children and even a perambulator for the new baby in the house), they are also generous with other things they can no longer use.

To introduce your family to skiing, it is advisable to let the children enjoy the snow. Norwegian children sometimes lie down flat on their backs in the snow and flap their arms and legs in great arcs. They call this action 'making angels' wings'. It is quite fun and the children will definitely enjoy it. Try it yourself. You might find yourself a quick convert to children's games in the snow.

## OTHER SPORTS

Norway offers not only winter sports. The country also gives unique opportunities for a wide range of outdoor summer sports. The most popular in Norway, as in most other European countries, is football, followed by handball. The latter is now mostly played indoors.

A characteristic aspect of sports in Norway is the mass participation. Most children participate in some sports activities, and it is this very broad base that makes it possible for the country to achieve top honours in international competitions despite its small population. If you are interested in participating, whether on a competitive level or just for the enjoyment, you should not have any problems in finding a club catering to your interest.

## NORWEGIAN NAMES

When you get to know Norwegian names, you might be struck by the similarities between surnames and place names. For example, a

Norwegian friend may be called Jorunn Nyttingnes, and one day, while on a bus travelling along the west coast, you find yourself passing a little town called Nyttingnes. You speak to your friend later and find out that she was born and grew up in that same little town. You wonder whether the town took its name from a distinctive family in the district or whether the family took its name from the place. More often than not, it is the latter.

In the old days, Norwegians were identified by their Christian name and their father's name: for example, Magnus Håkonson (or Håkonsson, the son of Håkon), Siri Håkonsdatter (or Håkonsdotter, the daughter of Håkon). In addition, a third name was very often used, usually a farm name. This 'surname' did not necessarily identify a family or a relationship: it often merely signified the dwelling place. When farmer Arne Pettersen Li moved from Li to another farm, e.g. Dale, he was called Arne Pettersen Dale. A farm labourer could be named in the same way, without being related to the farmer.

Sometimes, however, the preposition *på* (at) could be placed between the patronymic and the farm name, indicating that the person concerned had his occupation at that particular farm. Similarly, a tenant farmer (a cottager, *husmann*) was very often entered in the official register under the name of the farm to which his little home belonged, sometimes with the preposition 'under' before the name. Thus a cottager connected with the farm Heiberg could be called Harald Ivarsson Heiberg or sometimes Heiberg-eie (*eie* = possession), even if his home was commonly known by another name.

Today, however, the modern family name is quite a different matter. A surname in addition to the forename and the patronymic is not always the same as the modern family name. Family names in Norway are a product of only the last few generations, since it was only in 1925 that the use of fixed family names was made compulsory by law in Norway.

On emigrating, Norwegians sometimes bore a third name, perhaps the name of the farm which they had just left. Sometimes, they preferred to take the name of another farm they had lived at for some time, or adopted the name of their home parish. In some instances, they dropped the old farm name and used the patronymic as a family name. Ole Andersen and his son Anders Olsen could adopt the family name of Anderson or Olsen.

## Naming a Child

At a baptism ceremony of a Norwegian baby, you may find that the child is named after a living relative, usually either of the grandparents. In some Asian cultures, a child is never named after living relatives, since this meant that the child's parents are indirectly trying to hasten the demise of that relative so that their newborn child can take over its namesake's place. In Norway, however, grandparents are honoured and happy when their descendants are named after them.

In rural districts in Norway, there used to be very strict rules for naming children. The eldest son was named after his paternal grandfather and the second son after his maternal grandfather. The eldest and second daughters were similarly named after their paternal and maternal grandmothers. When the grandparents' names were used up, the great grandparents' names were the next to be used, though without strict rules as to the order. In some cases, special circumstances might interfere with these rules. Thus the name of a deceased spouse would be used first, and the name of the father or mother if the child was baptised after his or her death.

It was a saying that 'the name and the farm must go together'. For that reason, if a child had been earmarked as the next owner of the farm when he came of age, he was given the name of a previous owner, whether a relative or not. This was the custom in rural Norway many years ago. Today, however, Norwegians consult relatives or books of names for guidance. They pick names they like or are fond of, and sometimes name their children after their parents or grandparents. It is not unusual to find a grandparent's name as the middle name of a new child in the family.

# — *Chapter Two* —

# NORWEGIAN LAWS AND INSTITUTIONS

To get by in Norway one must be acquainted with its laws and institutions. The act of re-perceiving known and familiar concepts of, for example, marriage and child-rearing will open minds to new and unfamiliar ideas.

Knowledge of Norwegian laws and regulations eases cultural understanding and social mobility. It is always useful to be aware of the political and socio-cultural situation in a country before you embark on a discovery of the innate differences and perhaps tenuous similarities with your own culture. When you recognise and acknowledge the rules and laws that bind Norwegians together in a network of co-existence, you develop a perceptive sensitivity to the nuances that run along the boundaries defined by law and enforced by responsible acceptance.

Norway is a society that seems conservative and closed to some, open and liberal to others. Like other societies, it runs on the premise that there are rules to observe and follow. What is interesting is that in Norway, there is a degree of openness and accessibility that makes the dissemination and acquisition of information a relatively easy process – and this is despite the vast geographical diversity of the country.

If you are uncertain about what to do or where to go to do something in Norway, there are always government ministries or local departments you can contact to clarify your doubts. There is apparently nothing so secret that you cannot know about it. Norwegians expect a high degree of transparency from their government and they get it. They believe in sincerity and honesty and their government functions on this basic premise too. So if you do not understand something, ask and you will receive an answer. Hedging or evasion rarely happens.

Every citizen or resident in Norway has rights of access to information and clarification.

## NORWEGIAN LAW

Foreigners resident in Norway are subject to Norwegian law. All who commit an offence are punished in accordance with Norwegian law, and lack of knowledge of the law is no excuse. Therefore it is important to know the laws and regulations applicable in Norway.

### Punishable Offences Relating to...

*Children*: It is forbidden to physically punish children in Norway. Parents are not allowed to pull their children's hair in anger, hit them, or slap them. No corporal punishment is allowed at home, in school, or anywhere else.

*Women:* No one is permitted to strike a woman. Abuse of women at home or at work is frowned upon. Norway has legislation to protect women.

*Drugs and narcotics*: Import or sale of narcotics can result in imprisonment of up to 21 years. This is the longest prison term to which a person can be sentenced in Norway, and is the same as the maximum penalty for premeditated murder. Narcotics include marijuana, hash, amphetamines, cocaine, and heroin.

*Sexual Crimes:* There are strong penalties for sexual crimes, particularly for sexual relationships or offences concerning children under 16 years old.

## *Your Rights*

A number of basic rights apply to all who reside in Norway.

*Voting:* All Norwegians above the age of 18 have the right to vote in elections. Foreigners who have resided in Norway for at least 3 years have the right to vote in local elections.

*Freedom of speech:* Norway encourages freedom of speech and written expression. This means that all may speak or write critically of the government, for example, without punitive action being taken.

*Freedom of religion:* Those living in Norway have the basic right to practise their own religion. The majority of Norwegians are Lutherans and members of the Norwegian state church, but religious tolerance is part and parcel of living in Norway.

*Gender equality:* Norwegian law states that men and women are considered equal in all aspects of society. Women have the same rights as men, and all jobs are therefore open to women as well as men.

If a woman feels there has been sexist bias in the selection of a person for a job, she can voice her complaint and initiate an investigation. (This subject is discussed more fully in Chapter 8.)

*Children's rights:* Great emphasis is placed on the child's need for care, protection, and a good upbringing. Because Norwegian families are small and there are many single parents, the state plays an important role in the care of children and child welfare. Norway upholds the United Nations convention concerning the rights of children which states that all children have the right to be themselves, to feel safe in a family or with people who are taking care of them, and to learn that they are valued and equal members of society. (Chapters 5 and 8 expand on these subjects.)

## *AGE LIMITS*

It is useful to know the age limits that entitle young people in Norway to participate in certain activities. Cultural differences might make understanding certain privileges difficult, but awareness is the first step to take in clarifying issues.

Norway has well-defined rights for its citizens and residents. In 1992, its Department of Interpretation and Information in the Directorate of Immigration published a series of illustrative pamphlets that presented the different aspects of living in Norway, under the heading *For You – An Immigrant in Norway*. They covered several aspects, including housing, work and tax, education, and family. The following information comes from one of these pamphlets.

*5 years old*: Children 5 years old can go to the cinema to see special children's films.

*6 years old*: Children 6 years old can start school with the consent of the school board. As of 1992, some municipalities initiated pilot projects where school began at the age of 6.

*A Norwegian teacher welcomes her first-graders on the first day of school. She may follow them through three years as class teacher.*

*7 years old:* All children have the right and duty to start school.

*10 years old:* Parents are entitled to up to 10 days' leave from work when children under the age of 10 are sick. Single parents are entitled to 20 days' leave. Children between the ages of 5 and 10 can see young people's films when accompanied by an adult.

*12 years old:* Children 12 years old can state their opinion in cases that affect them, for example, when choosing which parent to live with if parents divorce. Children cannot be adopted without agreeing to it. Children shall be heard, as the saying goes, but they cannot decide for themselves. Twelve-year-olds have to pay the adult ticket fare for aeroplane flights.

*13 years old:* Children 13 years old can work at a light job that does not interfere with their schooling or affect their health. They can fill out their own income tax form for their own employment income.

*14 years old:* Children of 14 can hold a job as part of their educational or practical vocational training. Parents or legal guardians must take the young person's opinions into consideration in financial matters.

*15 years old:* Children of 15 have reached the age of criminal consent and are responsible for their actions. This means they can be arrested and punished for breaking the law. Special regulations exist concerning punishment for lawbreakers under the age of 15. Fifteen-year-olds have the right to choose the type of education they wish to pursue or the school they want to attend after their compulsory nine-year schooling. They can join or leave the state church, or other religious groups. By this age, children have the right to appeal any decision forced upon them by the child welfare authorities and can take such decisions before a court of law. The opportunity to work is greater, but overtime and night work are forbidden. They control their own income unless special considerations give a say to the guardian.

*16 years old:* Compulsory school attendance ends. Child welfare ends. Young people of 16 must have their own passports if they travel abroad. They are treated as adults on the bus, subway, and trains. They can obtain a driver's licence for light motorcycles (mopeds) and can purchase tobacco goods. Young people of this age can take a private criminal case to court in the event of assault and battery, and libel. From the age of 16 onwards, they are entitled to their own disability pension. They are over the age of sexual consent and can have sexual relations with people their own age and older. Girls and boys can sign on Norwegian ships sailing in domestic waters.

*17 years old:* Girls and boys can sign on Norwegian ships sailing in international waters.

*18 years old:* This is the age of majority. Eighteen-year-olds can now fully decide their financial and personal relations. They can marry

without their parents' consent. They can vote in national and municipal elections if they become 18 in an election year, even if their
birthdays fall after election day. As a rule, child support and child
pensions cease, but special arrangements can be made if, for example,
the young adult is going to college. Night work and overtime can be
taken on and 18-year-olds can write a will, purchase beer and wine,
and obtain a driving or weapons licence. Boys are summoned by the
military for a medical and are conscripted for military service. All 18-
year-olds can watch any film at the cinema.

Foreign nationals are allowed to vote in municipal and county
elections if they have lived in Norway over the last 3 years.

*19 years old:* Boys who are Norwegian citizens must serve in the
military, but can apply to have this postponed.

*20 years old:* They are allowed to purchase liquor.

*21 years old:* Care from the child welfare authorities ceases. Those
who were born disabled or became disabled before they reached 21
years of age are entitled to a minimum supplementary pension.

## CRIME AND VIOLENCE

Norway practises a liberal penalty system for most crimes. The
emphasis of the prison sentence is to bring the sentenced offender
back to society, to integrate him or her into the normal stream of social
life. In Norway, there is no corporal punishment such as caning. It
goes almost without saying that there is also no capital punishment in
Norway. Yet Norway has one of the lowest crime rates in the world.

There are many reasons for this phenomenon:

- An egalitarian system ensures a minimal gap between the haves
  and have-nots. In Norway, there are very few poor people. The
  society is broadly middle-class.
- The emphasis on social justice makes Norway and Norwegians

some of the most equitable administrators of justice. The society tries to uphold fairness and justice.

- Censorship of television programmes. This strict monitoring of television is an attempt to reduce the level of exposure, among TV viewers (especially children), to acts of violence. There is a theory that continued exposure to scenes of violence diminishes the viewer's sensitivity to violence, making him slowly immune to its horrors and more accepting of its atrocities. Norwegians are willing to permit sexually explicit scenes, to an extent, but refuse to relax their guard when it comes to censorship of TV violence.
- General self-respect and respect for other people and cultures. Norwegians are tolerant of differences, to a large degree, and relatively open to new influences (though sometimes this openness may vary from district to district). But what runs through all Norwegians is a sense of moral righteousness and respect for human dignity. Hence, Norwegians are always champions of human rights. This deeply-ingrained respect for people results in a generally anti-violent upbringing, which in turn is reflected in the character of individual Norwegians who seem calm, balanced, and dignified in difficult situations.

## TRANSPORTATION

In Norway, it is essential to have a car. Though the public transportation is efficient, it is still more convenient, especially if you have a family, to drive around Norway.

### Driving in Norway

One of the first things to do when you arrive in Norway is to convert your driving licence to a Norwegian one. The rules were tightened in October 1988, and now it is compulsory to sit for a '*glatt-före* (winter roads)' driving test. It operates on the assumption that some foreigners are not familiar with weather conditions in Norway. When it snows, roads become slippery and dangerous, thus learning to drive in winter conditions is an important requirement of anyone who holds a valid Norwegian driving licence.

Before the test, you have to take driving instruction, which is not cheap in Norway. Driving instructors charge about NOK120 (US$16.50) per hour. You need a certain fixed minimum number of lessons before you can qualify for the driving test. Success depends on your skill and confidence.

If you are the sort who panics and speeds as a result, then you are in trouble. You may wonder why your tester looks pale and grips the edge of his seat as you negotiate a dangerous snow-covered slope at 80 kmph! You think nothing of it and prepare to hear the good news. What you hear is that you have to spend more money and more time learning to drive in Norway.

Norway has good roads, but they also happen to be winding. When you drive up or down a mountain road, you will learn the true meaning of brinkmanship. As you attempt to negotiate your way up, you meet another car on its way down. What can you do? You can't back up all the way – the road is that far down! You look at the road in front of you and assess its width and potential. It only looks capable of accommodating one and a half cars, not two. You begin to despair and wonder why you ever took to driving in Norway. You could have learnt to cycle or lived near the sea instead of high up on the mountain.

If you study cars traversing a mountain road, you will notice that Norwegian drivers are a courteous race. They seldom honk their horns at each other and they take trouble to give way to each other. When it is a mountain road, the downgoing car will always swerve gently into the side of the road nearest the mountain side (usually there are little indentations for such a purpose) to make way for the upgoing car. If you are on the outside and you happen to look down, you might see sheer mountain and feel a little insecure about your manoeuvring. Take heart. The road is not as narrow as it appears. You can squeeze through, with room to spare.

Travelling along Norwegian roads gives a different perspective of time and space. As you take just 20 minutes to go from one small town to a bigger town nearby, you will marvel at the uncluttered nature of the roads. Imagine the insufferable traffic snarls in Bangkok or London, and the extensive amount of time needed to get from one part of the city to another in your own country. You begin to appreciate the spaciousness of Norway.

Country roads have very few traffic signs but there are distinct speed limits to observe. Expressways or motorways are mostly to be found in the direct vicinity of the cities, mainly in eastern Norway. You may be driving at a maximum speed of 80 kmph or 90 kmph on good mountain roads or expressways, but when you enter developed residential areas, the speed drops to 50 kmph – or less. The roads take care of 90% of all passenger traffic in Norway whereas sea transportation accounts for a substantial part of the movement of goods.

Car density is high. At 2.2 inhabitants per car, this corresponds to the density in France, Switzerland, Sweden, and Italy. However, there are few problems with road traffic density since Norway offers more roads per car and per inhabitant than any other European country.

## *Driving Under the Influence*

An important fact to note is Norway's very stringent laws concerning drinking and driving. Routine checks by police patrols are common. A driver of a motor vehicle with a blood alcohol concentration of more than the permissible limit of 0.05% can expect a severe penalty.

A driver with an alcohol percentage between 0.05% and 0.10% will generally receive a suspended jail sentence. If the percentage is between 0.10% and 0.15%, the jail sentence may or may not be suspended. A driver with an alcohol content of 0.15% or more will usually be imprisoned for at least 14 days. Penalties also include a larger fine, in addition to a jail sentence. The drunken driver's licence will be confiscated for a year or two. In some instances, the traffic police literally confiscate the licence from the offender on the spot.

There is talk of lowering the allowable alcohol limit even further.

## Ferries, Tunnels, and Bridges

The Norwegian road system has three special features: the extensive network of car ferries, road tunnels, and bridges across fjords. From Stavanger in the south to Honningsvåg and North Cape in the north, there are 230 regular scheduled ferry routes operating with remarkable regularity. The ferries are government-subsidised and fares are established by the authorities.

Boats and car ferries play a very important part in Norway's communication and transportation system. In Oslo and Bergen, a large part of suburban traffic is covered by boats and ferries.

To facilitate and speed up traffic, dozens of long tunnels, either through a mountain or under the sea, substitute a ferry service. On some tourist routes, the old road across the mountain is kept open during summer for nostalgic tourists. New bridges are being built across the fjords as Norway places priority on preserving the country's demographic structure. Consequently, there have been big public investments in regional roads and local infrastructure, perhaps at the expense of the cities. It is no surprise, therefore, to find a few toll stations on public roads, mainly to pay for a new bridge or a tunnel substituting a ferry service. Around Oslo and Bergen, toll stations collect money to pay for the construction of main roads and tunnels in the metropolitan areas, to minimise pollution and noise problems, and to improve the efficiency of transportation.

## Get Your Road Maps

Before motoring around Norway, get some motoring guides and maps, as well as lists of hotels and ferry timetables. Information pamphlets, printed by local tourist information offices, are distributed by information centres all over Norway. The Norwegian automobile associations have a very efficient information and service network. There are two associations: the larger Norges Automobil Forbund (NAF), with about 350,000 members, and the Kongelig Norsk Automobilforbund (KNA).

Make sure you purchase the most up-to-date road maps. In June 1992, all European motorways (except the E6 and E18) and about one-fourth of Norwegian secondary roads were assigned new route numbers. Under the new road plan, roads along the same route were assigned the same number in an effort to help drivers find their way more easily. On major roads, a new type of sign is now used. These roads have been assigned low numbers and signs are green. They are similar to the European motorway signs but lack the E before the route number.

## Express Bus

Taking an express bus is a pleasant alternative to train or car travel. An express bus system called Norway Bussexpress covers most longer stretches in Norway, including remote areas. In addition, several smaller local bus companies service most areas.

Riding on an express bus driven by someone who takes the curves and bends with dexterous ease and expertise is a relaxing exercise. The buses are all very comfortable, and coffee and tea are frequently provided free of charge.

You can check the bus routes by asking for a route guide or *rutehefte*. If you reside in Norway, bus and ferry route guides are delivered free of charge to your home. The times and dates scheduled are different for the summer and winter seasons so always check before you travel by bus or ferry.

## The Coastal Express

Because Norway's landscape is characterised by fjords and narrow straits, travelling by boat is common. If you want to travel to other towns in Norway, you have the choice of taking the bus or the boat. One popular and reliable express boat service that plies the coast of Norway is known as the Coastal Express.

The Coastal Express has become an institution in Norway, having been in operation for over 100 years. Eleven ships transport passengers and cargo all along the west and northwest coast from Bergen in southern Norway, via the North Cape, to Kirkenes near the Russian border. The round trip takes 11 days.

The four newest Coastal Express ships accommodate 40–50 private cars, which can be driven on board. The other ships only carry a few cars on deck. This can be an alternative for those who want to take the Coastal Express one way and enjoy the landscape by driving the other way. In the middle of summer, young people can travel very cheaply on these ships with a hiking ticket that is valid for one month.

## *Jetting Around Norway*

Norway's most important international airports are Fornebu and Gardermoen in the Oslo area, Flesland in Bergen, and Sola near Stavanger. You can travel directly to these airports from a number of European towns. Norway has a total of 58 airports, 19 of which belong to the regular network serviced by Scandinavian Airline System (SAS) and Bråthens SAFE. SAS is a Norwegian-Danish-Swedish partnership that is 50% government-owned.

Of the airports, 22 are exclusively government-owned, and 34 are owned and operated by others, including municipal authorities. During the late 1980s and early 1990s, considerable investments were made in modernising larger airports like Flesland and Sola. Major investments have been made at Fornebu and Vaernes (outside Trondheim). During the autumn of 1992, the Norwegian Parliament finally agreed, after several years of debate, to locate Norway's main airport at Gardermoen, 50 km north of Oslo. Construction work is expected to be completed in 1998 or 1999.

## *Getting on the Railway Track*

Norway has an excellent railway system that extends over 4,207 km, with more than 2,422 km serviced by trains run on electricity. The main railway lines branch out from Oslo to all the bigger towns in southern Norway and to Sweden, Denmark, and the Continent. From

Trondheim, the Nordland line continues across the Arctic Circle to Fauske, with connections to Bodø. Narvik, lying outside the rest of Norway's railway system, is linked up with Swedish railways (the Ofoten line). From Trondheim and from Oslo via Kongsvinger/ Charlottenberg and Halden/Kornsjø, there are connections to Sweden.

The Norwegian State Railway System (NSB) serves the express and longer lines as well as provides commuter service and local trains around Oslo, Bergen, and Trondheim.

In areas without railway services, NSB offers a range of bus services. The history of NSB dates back to 1854 when the first line was opened between Oslo and Eidsvoll, where the first Norwegian constitution was written in 1814. Bergensbanen (the Bergen line) was opened in 1909, after a 14-year battle with nearly impossible topographical conditions, a nasty climate, and huge amounts of snow in the winter.

Today, the highlight of train travel is to take the journey on the Bergensbanen between Oslo and Bergen – 1,301 metres above sea level, well above the tree line. This is a journey you should not miss, for its sheer excitement and the beauty of the landscape. For several hours, great electric locomotives pull the modern railway cars across a naked mountain plateau, crossing mountains through long tunnels, and crossing gorges over imposing bridges. The sideline down to Flåm at Sognefjord from Myrdal station has a general elevation of 55 degrees – one of the steepest railway lines in the world using normal trains – and some breathtaking tunnel turns.

NSB operates a range of European ticket-pass arrangements, e.g. Interrail, Nord-Tourist, Scanrail Pass, Eurail Pass, and Rail Europe Senior. Some of these rebates are valid only for Europeans, others for tourists from non-European countries. In any case, if you are over 67 years old, you will also enjoy the privileges that Norway extends to pensioners and senior citizens, including discounts of up to 50% on tickets on the public transport system.

## THE DISPENSARY – APOTEK

Doctors in Norway do not dispense drugs or medication. They only offer consultation and give you prescriptions that you take to the local dispensary. The chemists there will assemble the medication you need as you wait at the counter to collect it. The dispensary is marked by a sign announcing *Apotek*, the Norwegian equivalent of the English apothecary.

You can get vitamins at supermarkets, but if you need aspirin, cough mixtures, or some other medication, go to the *apotek*. If you live in a small town, the doctor at the local health station prescribes medicine. But if there is no local dispensary in the immediate locality, he will send your prescription to the nearest municipal dispensary. Your medication will arrive by boat or bus that evening and can be collected later at the health station or the cooperative supermarket known as *samvirkelag*. In the cities, there is always at least one *apotek* that is open 24 hours.

## NEWSPAPERS AND PARTY POLITICS

When you have become somewhat proficient in reading the Norwegian language, it is time to start reading one or more Norwegian newspapers. Norwegians read more than one newspaper to keep themselves informed of different points of view. Norway is a highly literate society and the number of newspaper and periodical copies per capita in Norway is among the highest in the world. Statistics indicate that 607 newspapers are sold per 1,000 inhabitants, putting Norwegians at the top of the list of newspaper readers, in front of Japan, Sweden, and Finland. Newspaper consumption is the equivalent of about 1.8 newspapers per household. Dailies represent 86% of total circulation. The average Norwegian over 15 years old spends nearly one hour a day reading printed matter other than books.

There are over 4,000 publications to choose from – compared with 60 newspapers and other publications in the 1850s, with a circulation of between 200 and 300. Today, the Magazine Publishers Association comprises 12 member organisations and commands an aggregate circulation per issue of 1.9 million.

Norwegian newspapers impress with their diversity and multiplicity. Few newspapers or periodicals are issued in Norway for purely economic reasons. In the early years, the motivation for publishing newspapers was economic and idealistic. Anyone who was devoted to a specific cause started a newspaper. For instance, in 1839, the Norwegian poet Henrik Wergeland founded the weekly *For Arbeidsklassen* (a magazine for the working class), which attained a circulation of 4,000. Wergeland's goal was the enlightenment of the general public. Political parties and organisations have sponsored the issue of newspapers and magazines since the late 1800s.

In Norway, many small newspapers are published at a large number of places. This geographical diversity can also be explained by Norway's topography and the special needs of small, isolated communities.

You will find that you have a choice between the national dailies, the regional newspapers, and the weekly magazines.

The two major national tabloids are *Dagbladet* (*The Daily Paper*) and *Verdens Gang* (*The Way the World Works*). In Bergen, the major daily is *Bergens Tidende* (*The Bergen Times*), a more serious and comprehensive regional newspaper. *Nationen* (*The Nation*) serves the agricultural sector while *Vårt Land* (*Our Land*) and *Dagen* (*The Day*) are Christian in orientation. Another paper catering to special interest groups is *Dagens Naeringsliv*, which is read by the shipping and commercial sector. *Arbeiderbladet* (*The Workers' Daily*) is the main labour-supported newspaper.

*Aftenposten* (*The Afternoon Post*) is Norway's biggest subscription daily and a national newspaper. *Aftenposten* was established by Christian Schibsted in 1860. It is an example of a newspaper concern that has been handed down within the same family – a natural consequence when the paper was a by-product of a family-owned printing works. The Schibsted consortium, which also issues *Verdens*

*Gang*, was registered on the Norwegian Stock Exchange in June 1992. Most papers have several owners, but compared with other countries, newspaper owners in Norway keep a fairly low profile and exert only moderate influence.

Only the very first newspapers were published in Norway with the prime aim of making money; they were mainly devoted to advertising. Norway's first newspaper, *Norske Intelligenz-Seddeler*, which began circulation in 1763, is one such example. *Addresseavisen*, which was first issued on 3 July 1767, is the oldest newspaper still printed in Norway that had its origins in the monetary motive. In the late 1800s, with the burgeoning economy and the growing number of printing works, Norwegian newspapers took off.

At that time, magazines with nationwide distribution were most widely read. Then several local newspapers started to appear. Heightened interest in politics was a stimulus to further reading, and from the 1870s, people spent more time reading newspapers than magazines. By 1910, the newspaper market was saturated and it was hard to find new reader groups, since Norwegians were by then already a nation of newspaper readers. The relationship between party politics and the press played a very important role in the development of politics and the publication industry. (A modern illustration of the close link between party and newspaper is in the Labour press, particularly in *Arbeiderbladet*, whose editor, until 1975, was chosen by the party.)

There is a dynamic interaction between the political source and the organ of publication. However, newspapers have never functioned simply as mouthpieces for their own party. Sometimes, it was the paper that influenced the party rather than the other way round. In debates, newspapers are usually open for contributions from all sides.

The political press has played a very active role in political development. It has also made newspaper readers and contributors participants in the process of political exchange and dialogue. It is a fact that Norwegian readers select a newspaper on the basis of political conviction.

## Weekly Magazines

In contrast to the newspapers, the weekly magazines in Norway have long enjoyed nationwide distribution. But like the papers, they aim for the broadest possible circulation – in all sectors of the community. It is in this aspect that the weeklies differ from the specialist press and other periodic publications.

Prior to 1870, the weekly magazines were more widely read than the newspapers. The magazines' governing principles were to encourage general enlightenment, impart practical knowledge, and tap the cultural life of the nation by featuring key cultural figures among their contributors.

Today, the highly illustrative nature of the news segments in these magazines, aided by advanced pictorial technology, enhances their cultural and entertainment value, making these magazines a popular reading choice in Norway. Many Norwegians subscribe to them; you might find yourself doing so too.

## Newspapers for Business and Trade

If you are a professional in Norway, you may find yourself reading some trade paper or other periodical.

The growth of large organisations from the end of the 19th century, bolstered by the need for professionalism and updates on the currency of new developments, were strong stimuli to publications of this type. For example, about 30 publications, with a total circulation of about 800,000 per issue, are linked to the trade unions. More than 500 magazines are issued by the churches or special religious affiliations, while 250 are company magazines. Winter sports, healthy lifestyles, the construction industry, and other special interest groups command a respectable figure in the publication industry.

The most widely read economic journal is probably *Kapital*, which gives in-depth journalism on economic and trade issues. It is on sale at newsstands.

## *Getting in Touch with the Press and Archives*

One interesting development is the Norwegian Telegram Bureau or *Norsk Telegrambyrå* (NTB) , a national news agency established in 1867, owned jointly by the major newspapers. You can use the NTB for research purposes when you need access to archival and historical photographs.

Journalists and other people interested in getting in touch with the media and having access to national newspapers and radio or television broadcasts from NRK and CNN, can visit the International Press Centre located in the Norway Information Centre, directly across from the Oslo City Hall. The International Press Centre on the first floor provides the following facilities and services for visiting journalists and correspondents based in Oslo:

• assistance in planning itineraries and interviews in Norway;
• work stations equipped with personal computers, typewriters and telephones;
• telefax and telex;
• free local calls, and payment (cash or card) for international calls;
• news service from the Norwegian News Agency (NTB);
• access to the Norinform database of information about Norway.

The Office of the Foreign Press Association in Norway is also located in the International Press Centre.

## *Professional Code of Press Ethics*

The press in Norway is independent of the government and enjoys a high degree of autonomy. There is no special press law in Norway, but this does not mean that the media can fire volleys of long shots at public newsmakers. A high degree of responsible reporting is expected and the press must observe and comply with the penal code, the public administration act, the freedom of information act, and the copyright act.

Anyone living in Norway has a right to information from any government department. There is no information that is barred from public knowledge. Similarly, the press expects access to all sources of information and maintains its right to freedom of expression. When news of the secret meetings, organised through the Norwegian government, between Israel and the Palestine Liberation Organisation (PLO) was revealed, the Norwegian press was somewhat surprised and a little peeved that such an act could have remained 'secret' to them for so long.

Interestingly enough, the Norwegian press imposes its own set of rules and regulations upon its practitioners. The main ethical guidelines are encapsulated in the 'Be careful' code adopted by the Norwegian Press Association in 1936, and more recently updated in 1987. These guidelines constitute the norm for press activity, many of them covering the protection of persons mentioned in news items. Another rule is that all sources must be protected and their anonymity respected if they so wish. Thus arises the phenomenon of seeing criminals giving voice to their opinions in the newspapers while the police are still hunting for them. Even when asked to collaborate with the public authorities and reveal the whereabouts of public criminals, the press will not budge on its protection of sources at whatever cost.

## RADIO AND TELEVISION

For about 50 years, the Norwegian Broadcasting Corporation (NRK) enjoyed an official broadcasting monopoly in Norway. Changes were first introduced through private local radio stations in 1981, and later with cable television channels. After several years of negotiation between political parties, TV2 – a new television station financed by advertisements, went on air during the summer of 1993. Prior to this, there had never been commercials or advertising on Norwegian television. Times have obviously changed.

In 1933, NRK was organised as an autonomous public corporation designed to 'establish and run stations and equipment for broadcasting announcements, photographs, etc.' NRK programmes are non-commercial and broadcasting is mainly funded by revenue from licence fees paid by the general public. In 1989, NRK became an independent foundation. However, the managing director is still appointed by the government. NRK still holds the lead in the number of viewers.

TV2, unlike the non-profit NRK, has problems competing with popular cable channels like TV Norge and Nordic TV3 for commercial revenue from advertisements. Norwegians are today also bombarded by cable television like Filmnet and other foreign satellite television. There is considerable choice for television viewers in Norway, but Norwegians are not television addicts yet because their lifestyles are oriented towards the outdoors.

## *DEFENCE AND NATIONAL SERVICE*

You are unlikely to be affected by conscription into national service. However, knowing how the general defence system works in Norway is learning about the Norwegian concept of military service and Norway's peace-loving nature. The main objectives of the Norwegian Armed Forces are to maintain peace through preventive action and to secure the freedom of the government to assert the rights and interests of the Norwegian people in times of peace. Norwegian defence is based on compulsory basic military training for all men. Women may voluntarily participate in military training and go for a professional military education.

In May 1992 the Storting re-evaluated and ratified the principles of compulsory military service. Economic difficulties and stricter quality requirements resulted in varying periods of compulsory service: 12, 9, or 6 months. (In earlier years, all young Norwegian men went through 18 months of military service.) Following initial service, some soldiers are retained on military registers until they reach the age of 44. Reserve officers remain on call until the age of 55. Refresher training exercises are held regularly, but increasingly tight budgets have resulted in cutbacks. The defence budget in 1993 was 22,5 billion NOK, or about 6.5% of the entire national budget.

It is Norwegian policy to hold allied training exercises annually in Norwegian territory, on land or at sea. Increased Norwegian participation in the United Nations Peace Keeping Forces is also planned. In the beginning of 1993, Norwegians were active in peace-keeping forces in Lebanon, Kuwait/Iraq, the former Yugoslavia, Angola, and Somalia. More than 40,000 Norwegians have participated in United Nations activities since the organisation was founded.

Apart from the army, navy, and air force, Norway also maintains the Home Guard or National Guard corps, a lightly equipped, decentralised force designed for rapid mobilisation. Units based on a model used by the resistance movement during World War II are prepared to take control of important installations and secure mobilisation of other branch forces on short notice.

The Military Service Act was passed in 1854, but military service was not made compulsory until 1876. Today's system of military service is based on the Military Service Act and the Home Guard Act, both adopted in 1953. In an amendment to the Acts in 1979, women who volunteer to serve in the Armed Forces become subject to the same rules for mobilisation and service as men. This represents the extent to which gender equality is observed in Norway.

Normally, military service starts during the year a male Norwegian citizen reaches 19 years of age, and lasts to the end of the year he reaches 44 years. The service includes a period of initial service, refresher training, and possible additional service in peacetime. In addition, there is the obvious service obligation if the Armed Forces are mobilised. Exemptions from serving in the Armed Forces are made for conscripts who do not satisfy the medical requirements of fitness, whose usefulness in the Armed Forces is limited, and who refuse to serve in the army because of conscientious objections, which could be religious, ethical, or political.

Norway is relatively tolerant of young men who object to the whole concept of military service because of their personal ethical beliefs. As long as the conscript can demonstrate the validity of his objections before a committee, he will be released from military service to perform civilian service in the health and social work sectors, or in some humanitarian organisations. Some young men have served as kindergarten teachers as part of their civilian service. The figure of exemptions from military service number about 2,000 to 2,500 every year.

## THE CONSTITUTIONAL MONARCHY

Norway is a constitutional monarchy closely interwoven with the concept of political democracy governing the country. What this means is that the king is selected by the Storting, and the constitution stands above the king.

With its famous resolution of 7 June 1905, the Storting unilaterally deposed the Swedish king (see *The Royal Family*, below), but at the same time, it firmly placed the monarchy within a wider framework that reduced kingly power but simultaneously gave the monarchy greater legitimacy.

The monarchy is legally rooted in the first section of the Norwegian constitution where Norway is defined as 'a Kingdom' with a 'limited and hereditary monarchy'. This means that the monarchy can only be abolished by law, through an amendment to the constitution. It seems rather odd that a modern society like Norway should adhere to the antiquated system of monarchy. What must be understood is the idea that the king is a representative of the people who give him legitimacy. The monarchy is a framework, not a brake, for the process of democratisation. The monarchs of modern Norway, King Håkon (who ruled from 1905 to 1957), King Olav (1957–91), and King Harald (1991–), chose as their motto, *Alt for Norge* (All for Norway).

Even though the king today has very little direct political power, a great majority of the population wish to maintain the monarchy. A proposal to abolish the monarchy is regularly tabled in the Storting, but this virtually compulsory exercise on the part of the republicans is scarcely taken seriously, even by them. The people's desire to

*King Olav was a navy man and a keen sailor. Much admired and respected, he will always be remembered as the people's king.*

continue with the monarch as head of state is due to the great popularity of the royal family and the fact that it was the nation's symbol of unity during World War II.

King Håkon's resounding 'No' to German demands on 10 April 1940 stands sharply illuminated in the history of the monarchy and of Norway. The Germans had wanted to install a puppet government in Norway headed by a man called Quisling. But the king refused to

71

acknowledge this act. His statement to the government was, 'The decision is yours. But if you choose to accept the German demands, I must abdicate.'

## THE ROYAL FAMILY

From 1814 to 1905, there was a union between Norway and Sweden – through the Swedish king. When Norway broke away from the union in 1905, a Danish prince, Prince Carl, was asked to become Norway's king. He accepted and took the name of Håkon VII. King Håkon arrived in Norway in 1905. When he died in 1957, the entire country mourned.

When his son, King Olav, died in January 1991, loyal followers gathered in front of the Royal Palace in Oslo, placing lighted candles in the snow to his memory. King Olav had always been known as a king of the people – he had a gift for relating to the ordinary people, which endeared him to them.

King Olav's son took over the throne, and was crowned Harald V. When Harald was born, it was the first time in 567 years that a prince had been born in Norway. In 1968, while he was still Crown Prince, Harald married Sonja Haraldsen, a commoner. The royal couple have two children – Princess Martha Louise (born 1971) and Crown Prince Magnus (born 1973).

### Rights of Succession

According to the constitution, Norway has a linear succession and the right of succession was previously also agnatic, meaning that the oldest legitimate 'man born of man' inherited the throne. The constitution has now been changed so that women can also accede to the throne, but as an interim arrangement, it was decided that the male line should have precedence for those children born before 1990. In practice, this means that Princess Martha Louise, who is two years older than her brother, would only accede to the throne if her brother were to die without having any children or grandchildren.

*King Harald ascended the throne on the death of his father, King Olav V, on 17 January 1991. Like his father and his grandfather, King Håkon VII, he adopted the motto, 'All for Norway'.*

## The Royal Lineage

As an illustration of the Norwegian fondness for passing on names of their ancestors to their children, let us look at how Princess Martha Louise was named. Her namesakes were her grandmother, Crown Princess Martha, wife of King Olav V, and her great-great-grandmother, Queen Louise, mother of King Håkon VII and daughter of Carl XV of Sweden.

The Norwegian royal family has close ties to the Danish, Swedish, and British royal families. King Håkon VII was the second son of King Frederik VIII of Denmark. His wife, Queen Maud, mother of King Olav, was the daughter of King Edward VII and Queen Alexandra of England. King Olav's wife, Martha, was the second daughter of Swedish Prince Carl and Princess Ingeborg.

## The Role of the Royal Family

Members of the royal family have been very good ambassadors for Norway internationally and take an active part in promoting the export of Norwegian goods. They also enjoy a special position in the hearts of the Norwegian people, particularly because of their relentless loyalty to the cause of freedom under German oppression and occupation during World War II.

The king also perhaps plays the role of father, as the king in fairytales, who fulfils the common need for fantasies and also for identification. He symbolises unity in the midst of political confusion, neutralises and subdues sectoral strife, and is the focal point far removed from sector interests.

The Norwegian royal family has traditionally brought up their children as far as possible in the same way as other Norwegians. Their children attended local schools and were not given special treatment. Many people believe this is one of the reasons why the royal family is so popular in Norway. They are part of the people.

## Sports and the Royal Family

The representativeness of the Norwegian royal family is a strong point in its favour. The king and queen and their children enjoy hobbies that are typically Norwegian in character.

Sports play a significant role in the lives of Norwegians, so too in the daily lives of the royal family. King Olav won an Olympic gold medal for sailing in 1928 and was an active sailor all his life. He was also an enthusiastic ski-jumper and took part in many competitions,

Holmenkollen being one of them. King Harald is also a first-class sailor, and is especially proud of his 1987 World Championship victory in the 1-tonne class. When the Olympic Games were opened in Lillehammer in Norway, Crown Prince Magnus received the Olympic torch from the final runner and ran up the steps to light the Olympic fire. He is also an active sportsman while his sister Princess Martha Louise is a competent equestrienne.

## THE NOBEL PEACE PRIZE

Norway takes centrestage in the international arena in October, when the names of the Nobel prize winners are announced to the world. The first Nobel prize was awarded in 1901. There are five Nobel prizes for significant contributors in the fields of physics, chemistry, physiology or medicine, literature, and peace.

Alfred Nobel was a Swede, and it seems strange that he should have made a will in 1895, stipulating that the scientific prizes and the prize for literature should be awarded by Swedish institutions while the decision regarding the peace prize was to be left to a committee appointed by the Storting in Norway. Perhaps Nobel had great respect for the work of the Norwegian Storting in international politics, for example its 1880 decision in favour of international arbitration. Or perhaps his will was a personal attempt to give redress to a nation that struggled and agitated for a dissolution of the union with Sweden towards the end of the 19th century. Another reason could be that Nobel was more of a European than a provincial Swede, having lived outside Sweden most of his life.

Whatever his reasons for this division of responsibility for awarding the Nobel prizes, the fact is that Norway is entasked with the important duty of identifying and selecting a winner for the Nobel peace prize every year. The Storting appoints the five members of the Peace Prize Selection Committee, but this does not imply that it is responsible for the committee's decisions. The committee is a completely independent body. Prize winners include public figures such as Albert Schweitzer (1953), Martin Luther King (1964), Menachem Begin (1978), Mother Teresa (1979), the 14th Dalai Lama (1989), Mikhail Gorbachev (1990), and Aung San Suu Kyi (1991).

To be valid, nominations have to be submitted by 1 February of the year for which the prize is being awarded. Peace prizes may be awarded to institutions or organisations, as well as to individuals. For example, UNICEF was awarded the prize in 1965, and more recently, the United Nations Peace Keeping Force, in 1988. The Peace Prize has been awarded only 70 times since 1901; no award was given on 19 occasions. These interruptions have been mainly due to the two world wars and to the fact that in peacetime, the committee has frequently been unable to arrive at a positive decision.

The award ceremony takes place on 10 December, the anniversary of Alfred Nobel's death, and ceremonies are held on that date, both in Stockholm and Oslo. Since 1945, nearly all prize winners have attended the award ceremony, always held in the presence of the Norwegian king. The king, however, does not present the prize as in Stockholm. In Oslo, this task is performed by the chairman of the committee, an act that again testifies to the judicious exercise of power and authority on the part of the Norwegian monarch.

## GOVERNMENT AND POLITICS

The Norwegian Parliament (Storting) comprises 165 members who are elected for a four-year period. During that period, it cannot be dissolved, nor can a new election be called, as is the case in many other countries. The Storting is divided into 13 permanent committees, covering the various main fields of work. In plenary meetings, matters are settled after one reading. In the passing of laws, a different routine is followed. The Storting is subdivided into two bodies (houses), the Odelsting and the Lagting; bills must be passed by both in succession, and signed by the king of Norway, before a law becomes operative.

In Norway, there is universal franchise for all citizens from the age of 18. Elections are held every two years. These include the general elections to the Storting every four years and local elections to the county and municipal councils every two years. Parliamentary elections were held in 1993 and will next be held in 1997, while municipal and county elections will be conducted in 1995 and 1997.

If you have been resident in Norway for the previous three years, you are eligible to vote at the municipal and county elections. You might find yourself noticing that different counties do not have the same number of representatives in Parliament: Finnmark has 4 representatives, for example, whereas Oslo has 15. The relative number of inhabitants is larger in small counties. In Oslo, about 30,000 voters back each representative while the number in Finnmark is about 20,000 – i.e., Finnmark is over-represented in terms of parliamentary seats.

The government of Norway consists of 19 ministers, including the prime minister. The ministers each head their own ministry. Two ministers (Development Cooperation and Trade) head departments in the Ministry of Foreign Affairs, and two ministers share the Ministry of Health and Social Affairs (one handles health matters and the other handles social matters). The ministries are: Finance; Government Administration; Industry and Energy; Justice and Police; Education, Research and Church Affairs; Agriculture; Cultural Affairs; Environment; Transport and Communications; Health and Social Affairs; Fisheries; Defence; Local Government and Labour; Children and Family Affairs; Foreign Affairs; Trade (and Shipping); and Development Cooperation.

Gro Harlem Brundtland became Norway's first woman prime minister in 1981. However, election that year brought a government led by Kåre Willoch of the Conservative Party to power. Brundtland became prime minister again in 1986, and has since held the post, except for a short break in 1989. Known internationally as the 'World's Minister of the Environment', Brundtland has drawn attention to the need for international monitoring and enforcement of environmental protection. When the UN General Assembly decided

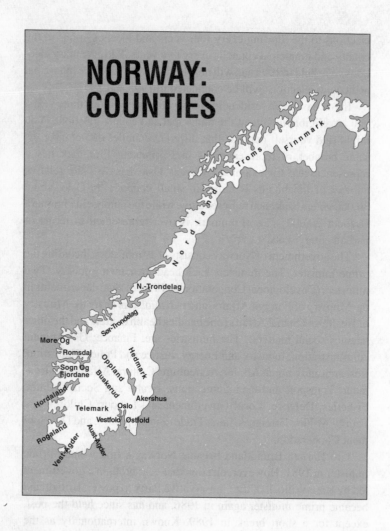

in autumn 1983 to establish the World Commission on Environment and Development, she was appointed to chair this commission, which included members from 21 other countries.

## Political Parties

Eight political parties are represented in the Storting. The two largest are the Labour Party and the Centre Party. The others are the Christian Democratic Party, the Conservative Party, the Leftwing Socialist Party, the Rightwing Progressive Party, and a protest party called Progress for Finnmark.

## County and Municipal Administration

Norway is divided into 18 counties, inclusive of the capital Oslo, which is a separate county. The county administration serves as a coordinating link between the central and local governments. Its direct administrative responsibility includes upper secondary school education, transport, hospitals, and the more specialist health and psychiatric care.

As at April 1993, Norway had 439 municipalities. Each municipal council collects taxes within boundaries that are prescribed by the Storting. Among its responsibilities are schools up to primary and secondary levels, social and health services, churches, roads, water, sewerage and electric systems, the firefighting service, and general planning.

Forty-six municipalities have urban status. In some of these, urban neighbourhood committees have been set up. The number of urban neighbourhood committees ranges from 35 in Oslo to 4 in Notodden. The first of these was appointed in Oslo in 1972. The role of the committee is in keeping with the spirit of decentralisation, drawing people into the ongoing political process whereby they give their opinions on local matters, administer funds for social and cultural activities, and take care of certain administrative tasks.

# Chapter Three

# LIVING IN NORWAY:
# SETTLING IN

When you arrive in Norway, you are surprised, excited, bewildered. The country seems so vast, the mountains may dominate the landscape everywhere you turn, and the people dwarf you. The weather is unpredictable, but the food is palatable. Greatly encouraged, you set out on your first task, looking for the place you will call home for the next few years.

## *FINDING ACCOMMODATION*

When you arrive in Norway, you may initially stay at the hotel near your work place, but you are on the lookout for a more settled home.

Most Norwegians own their own homes, but in the cities and towns, where housing is rather expensive, it is not unusual to rent a home. Foreigners who relocate to Norway can find accommodation in several ways; it all depends on who your employer is. A private corporation may have housing for its own employees at either subsidised or market rates. If you are on your own, contact rental agencies and read the advertisements. As these are in Norwegian, you would need a Norwegian friend to interpret. You could advertise: four or five lines will cost about NOK100.

You could also use notice boards to announce that you are looking for a place to live. Try the local provision stores, library, doctor's surgery, post office, and other public places. A notice may be put up free of charge. You could also put up a notice at your place of work.

If you want to know how to find accommodation in Norway, the Directorate of Immigration has an informative brochure on housing, from which the following facts have been extracted.

## Rented Housing

Flats (*leiligheter*) for rent are found in apartment blocks and apartment houses, and sometimes in private houses. Rented apartments may be furnished or unfurnished.

The landlord has to ensure that the apartment is in good condition when you move in. It must be clean and have keys to all external doors. If you find the state of the apartment unsatisfactory, inform the landlord of this within 14 days. The landlord is also responsible for seeing that the cellar, the stairways, and the loft or attic are clean and adequately lit, unless the contract specifically mentions that this is the tenant's responsibility. Normal wear and tear is covered by the normal rent. You are not required to cover larger expenses, for example, the cost of a new hot water tank or electrical installations. If you wish to undertake major improvements to the apartment yourself, you should contact the landlord first to negotiate a written agreement so that you can recover some of these expenses when you move out.

If you are moving into a rented apartment, make sure there is a written contract binding on both parties. The Norwegian Tenants' Association (*Norges Leieboerforbund*), Juss-Buss, and the Office for Free Legal Aid can all assist in advising you whether the contract is legal. The Immigrant and Refugee Housing Association (SIFBO) supplies a standard contract in several languages; you can purchase this contract in Norwegian in a bookshop.

When you move out, you should leave the apartment clean and in its original condition. If you have no time to clean the premises before you leave, the landlord may employ a cleaner to tidy up after you and you will be expected to pay the cost.

The rent is usually paid on the first of the month. You have the right to demand a receipt for the rent paid. If you have reason to believe that the rent is excessive, you may contact the rent tribunal (*husleienemnd*), if there is one in your local authority. The tribunal will determine the maximum rent that may be charged for a specific apartment. If there is no local rent tribunal, you may contact the Price Inspectorate (*Statens pristilsyn*), which has regional offices throughout the country.

You are expected to pay a deposit not exceeding the equivalent of six months' rental when you rent an apartment. This money is placed in a closed bank account and is security for the landlord as a precaution against non-payment of the rent, or for costs incurred if the apartment is vacated without being cleaned. If the landlord has no expenses he may legally deduct when the tenant moves out, the deposit must be repaid in full, with interest.

If you are given notice to vacate the apartment, this must be in writing. It must be validated and should not be unreasonable. For bedsitters and small apartments not exceeding two rooms, the normal notice required is one month; for larger apartments, notice must be at least four months. If you do not accept the reasons for being given notice, you must make an objection immediately, preferably within one week.

There are other types of contracts. A contract may relate to a specific period, for example in the case of service accommodation rented out by a firm to an employee as part of an employment contract. This has to be vacated when you leave the job.

Sub-letting an apartment from a person who has rented it directly from the landlord carries a risk. If the person from whom you rented the apartment is given notice, this applies automatically to you as well. Normally, sub-letting is for a fixed period only.

## Renting from the Local Authorities

Some local authorities have accommodation for rent that is available for a limited period. It may be especially intended for young persons living on their own. The local authority has specific requirements – regarding the age and income of the applicant, for instance. The authority's housing office or social welfare office will supply information on request.

## Bedsitters

A bedsitter (*hybel*) – a single room, usually with the use of the kitchen and bathroom – is popular with singles, particularly college students. Whole apartment blocks of bedsitters exist but most bedsitters are found in private houses. Basically, a bedsitter is a room for rent. It is nearly always fully furnished, but once requested by the house-owner to move out, you have to do so without demurring.

Hostels and boarding houses also rent rooms, normally on a nightly basis. If you must stay in a hostel, make it a short stay as it can be expensive. The standard of the rooms vary.

## Student Accommodation

Special student accommodation is found at all universities and most colleges (*högskoler*), but there are not enough apartments for all students. Student hostels usually involve communal living, where each student has his or her own room, and shares the kitchen and bathroom with others. There are also apartments for married students and couples living together, with or without children. Contact the student welfare association (*student-samskipnader*) or a welfare organisation at the institution for more information.

## Housing Cooperative

Many people in urban areas live in housing cooperatives (*borettslag*). A housing cooperative often consists of a number of apartment blocks or small houses. A deposit or share (*innskudd*) must be paid before you can move in. In addition, you pay rent each month. If you want to have more permanent housing and own it, you can join a cooperative.

The Norwegian Federation of Cooperative Housing and Building Associations, NBBL (*Norske Boligbyggelags Landsforbund*), has a list of all the cooperatives in Norway. You can enrol as a member and pay an annual membership fee. You can also save money in an account managed by the cooperative while you are waiting for housing built by it to be available.

The deposit must be paid before you move into your apartment. At the same time, you become a shareholder and are responsible for the loan that the cooperative has taken out. The price of these apartments is therefore the sum of the deposit and the share of the common debt. The rent is used to repay the joint loan the cooperative took out in order to build the apartments. Part of the rent is also used for expenses like the maintenance insurance on the buildings, and the communal washroom. You cannot be given notice to vacate the apartment as long as you pay the rent regularly and follow the bylaws of the cooperative.

If you want to move out, you can sell your share in the cooperative. Normally, people already living in the cooperative will have first priority. You can also rent out one or more rooms. The board of the cooperative must always approve any contract concerning the letting of rooms or sale of the apartment.

### Estate Agents

If you want to buy a house, you can do so through an estate agent or a lawyer's office. This act involves certain fees. If you decide to circumvent the estate agent, you should have the property evaluated by an authorised assessor. You should also always investigate whether there are outstanding debts on the property or buildings. This means checking if the previous owner has taken out a mortgage on the property as security for a loan, for example. The district judge's office (*sorenskriver*) has a register of such transactions.

### Moving Out – Flytting

When you move house, you are obliged by law to inform the Population Registry (*Folkeregister*) found in every local authority or municipality within eight days after moving. This rule applies even if you move house within the same municipality or to another apartment in a housing cooperative. When moving to another municipality, you should inform the registry at the previous locality.

### Insurance – Forsikring

The most common types of housing insurance include:

- Property insurance (*huseierforsikring*) which covers damage to buildings. If you live in a cooperative or apartment building, insurance premiums of this type are automatically included in the monthly rent.
- Domestic insurance (*hjemforsikring*) is essentially for persons living in all types of rented accommodation. This insurance covers furnishings and personal property where damage is caused by fire, water, or burglary. Everyone is required to have this form of insurance.
- House insurance (*villaeierforsikring*) covers the building and its contents, and is especially suited to persons owning their own house. If you have a mortgage on your house, the bank will require that you have this form of insurance as well as life insurance.

If you have electrical appliances or equipment purchased outside Norway, check at the offices of the local electricity company for approval. If a fire occurs as a result of equipment that has not been approved, the insurance company will not pay compensation.

Make sure water pipes are well insulated. If you are absent for any length of time in winter, the water pipes should be drained and the water supply closed.

## MOVING DAY BLUES

At last you have found a place to live – you will be moving out of the hotel or *pensjonat* (an inexpensive motel) into your own apartment or house. You've got the keys. Your bags are packed.

You are in your new home. It may be a simple abode or a large house. The only thing is, the lights seem to be all missing. There are loose ends of wires dangling from the ceilings and the walls where you expect to find them. But there is no electricity. You happen to have rented an unfurnished house.

You want to wash the floors in preparation for moving in. (Actually, the floors seem quite clean but you will wash them anyway because your mother taught you that floors of new homes should always be washed before moving in.) You fill a bucket with water. You start scrubbing away faithfully, and gasp. The water is cold, ice-cold. It is the dead of winter, and you have forgotten to tell the electricity department in the municipality to switch on the electrical supply for your house. Very soon, your hands have forgotten they belong to you because you can't feel them anymore.

The first thing you learn is that, when you wash the floor with your hands, you use a mop or don rubber gloves to protect your hands. Even if you are not a mollycoddled townie, remember that hands tend to get dry in the Norwegian climate. You would do well, particularly if you come from a more humid climate, to buy hand cream for your hands and lip gloss to protect those cracking lips. The dry weather in Norway is unkind to skin, which needs to be protected.

*A Norwegian neighbourhood has lots of space for children and no fences.*

## Ask the Neighbour

After you have asked yourself for the hundredth time why you moved to Norway in the winter (forgetting you had no choice), you set to wondering how you can get some lights into the house. Your best bet is your next-door neighbour. Asking for help is always a good ice-breaker, a means of saying 'Hello. I'm the new neighbour in the block who didn't know there would be no electricity and no hot water in the house before I moved in. Hello.'

If your neighbour is also a foreigner, that is fine because you can find out all the problems and joys of being a foreigner living in Norway – within the two hours the neighbour has you over for tea. Whatever the case might be, call on your neighbour.

## Get Me Some Light!

Going back to your original problem: why are there no lights in your new home? The switches are all in place. The wires are all there. But the lamps are glaringly missing.

What has happened is that the last tenant took all the lamps away. But before you go off in hot pursuit of those 'thieves', you had better know a few things about moving into a new home.

In Norway, it is accepted that when you move into your 'unfurnished' residence, you provide your own lamps and other necessities. Only rented property that comes 'furnished' has lamps in the necessary places, otherwise the only fixtures provided are the sockets in the walls and the wires. Thus, one of the first things to do before you move into a house or apartment in Norway is to buy some lamps.

Electricity costs a pittance, compared to places like England. An advertisement on energy conservation in Norway some years back featured a building with all its lights on in the different empty offices after office hours. Seeing this, the Britons shook their heads and said, "It must be Norwegians occupying that building."

## GET TO KNOW IKEA!

A good place to shop for reasonably-priced furniture, including basic electrical items, is IKEA. This Scandinavian department store chain catering to all domestic needs began as an inexpensive alternative to Scandinavian furniture shops that were burning the pockets of the average householder in Norway. IKEA is a Swedish chain recognised worldwide.

Within Norway itself are other Scandinavian furniture stores that do not enjoy IKEA's international repute, but have its own regional market in Norway. These are the furniture supermarkets, also known as *varehus*. On the west coast of Norway, Møbelhuset is a good example of a region-based *varehus* of reliable repute.

## INSTALLING A FIRE ALARM

Those who come from some countries in Southeast Asia or the Middle East are not used to the idea of having a fire alarm in the house. In Norway, however, it is the accepted practice to have fire alarms or smoke detectors installed in different parts of the house, especially the kitchen and bedrooms. Most Norwegian houses are of wood, and kitchens are a very vulnerable part of the house because of cooking over stoves and accidental fires. Old people who are forgetful and leave the ovens on can also start fires. Whatever the reason, it is a sensible precaution to have fire alarms in the home.

On 1 August 1979, Norway took measures to ensure that fire alarm systems marketed for the home met national standards and regulations. From that date, it became illegal to sell fire alarms not recognised by the State Institute for Radiation. When you buy your fire alarm from the local electrician, make sure it specifies the following: the State Institute for Radiation; approved registration number; model number; and manufacturer's name.

It is usually smoke that kills. Smoke detectors or fire alarms correctly placed in private residences can save lives. In Norway, approximately 70 people die in fires every year – about 80% of them from asphyxiation. All fires produce flammable gases that are poisonous and explosive. The most common and dangerous of these is tasteless, invisible, and odourless carbon monoxide. A good smoke detector will smell out invisible gases at a very early stage – in enough time for the family in the house to be forewarned and evacuated if necessary. Moreover, the fire can be put out in good time.

You must place your smoke detector in the ceiling so it can react immediately to fire gases. The distance from the alarm to the wall must be at least 50 cm. Place the fire alarm such that it can be heard from the bedrooms or in the corridor between the rooms. To ensure better protection, place an alarm in the cellar and near the staircase to the first floor. Think also of the other rooms susceptible to fire – the sitting room, where the fireplace is, and the TV room. To test the alarm, blow smoke into it. If you want to know where to locate your several fire alarms, contact the fire department.

From 1990, by law all households had to have fire-fighting equipment, such as a fire hose or fire extinguisher. Check with your Norwegian neighbour or the police department if you are not sure.

## *TUMBLE-DRY YOUR WORRIES AWAY*

A Norwegian male is very fond of things electrical. He will amaze you with his knowledge of state-of-the-art domestic electrical connections and how things work at home. A Norwegian woman will be most helpful in volunteering pots and pans and other essentials for the kitchen or bedroom if she knows you are shorthanded. You may borrow blankets or quilts, woollens for your children, scarves for yourself, and maybe even get to use the neighbours' washing machine – and tumble-dryer!

You will soon learn the advantages of having a tumble-dryer, especially if you have children and lousy weather for drying clothes outdoors. In winter, be careful if you want to dry your clothes outside. There is an advertisement for a brand of detergent that demonstrates how rival detergents produce laundry so starched and stiff, they stand up straight on their own. That is the laundry you will be taking in if you dry your clothes out in freezing temperatures.

## *GETTING TO KNOW* OMGANGSSYKDOM

Norway is a land of four seasons. When one season moves into the next, there is a natural transition of change. The air changes, the flowers blossom or wither, depending on whether it is spring or winter. Children and adults react to the seasonal change, which brings with it pollen in the air and bacteria floating around, and sometimes they come down with this strange sickness characterised by stomach-ache, diarrhoea, occasional vomiting, and a rippling queasiness in their stomach that seems to imitate the movements of a snake coiling and uncoiling itself in the inner recesses. Sometimes the victims suffer a mild fever attack.

Do not panic. Call for the doctor if you will. He will probably diagnose *omgangssykdom*, which is nothing really serious. The treatment is to ingest an ugly, black liquid that your child is guaranteed to hate until you tell him it will get rid of that snake in his stomach. This is *kull* or liquid charcoal, and it works. Believe me, it works fast.

Before long, your child will be back to normal and be the active little rascal he was before he got stricken. Three cheers for *kull*!

A note about *omgangssykdom* – It comes at the turning point of every season, so do not be upset if you find yourself coming down with this ailment at the start of every season. Simply keep a bottle of *kull* in your medicine cabinet – it always comes in handy.

## DRINKING WATER

If you live in the countryside, you might find yourself going on walks in the mountains, enjoying the scenery. If it is autumn, you will find blueberries growing haphazardly and discover the joy of plucking them straight from the bushes to pop into your mouth. And when you get thirsty, you can go to the nearest stream and collect mountain water in your cupped hands to drink.

Most of the water that comes down the mountain in streams is pure and safe to drink. If you have seen the translucence of melted ice water from the glaciers, you will notice the emerald-green colour of the water higher up in the mountains. It becomes blue and light the further down it travels. Its colour is very much dependent on its temperature.

In Norway, the water that issues from taps can also be drunk. There is no need to boil the water, yet boiling water to kill bacteria remains a habit among the people of some cultures. Norwegians see foreigners boiling water and cannot understand when told it is for drinking. Norwegians boil water only to make a hot drink.

If you are cautious about drinking water directly from the tap, get a water filter to strain out impurities. You can attach this piece of equipment to the tap or fix it somewhere to the sink, and feel safer. If it is your custom to boil water, continue doing so. If you are a guest in a Norwegian home, you should remember that Norwegians use tap water to dilute cordial concentrates, and tap water is often served as drinking water at the dinner table. Be frank if you worry about drinking unboiled water. They will give you juice or a hot drink instead.

## WASHING DISHES – YOUR TURN, DEAR!

If you have children, washing dishes can mean incessant drudgery at the sink. It can also mean damaged hands or chapped fingers. Wise up and do what the Norwegians do: invest in a dishwasher. The dishwasher must have been created for large families and working parents: it is a solid investment that can save you time to expend on other more worthwhile projects than mere routine at the sink.

Norwegian taps come as a pair – one for hot water and the other for cold. The sink comes as a double unit too. Do not be surprised if your Norwegian friend volunteers to do the dishes at the sink (if, regrettably, you do not have a dishwasher) and you see him doing something you normally would not do. He washes the dirty dishes in one sink to get the surface dirt off, and then puts them in the other sink that has been filled with a warm soapy detergent solution. He scrubs the dishes with a brush, rinses them in the soapy water, then takes them out of the water, still dripping soap, and places them on the dish rack to dry.

If you are used to rinsing off soap from dishes under running water or in a sink of clear water, you might be a bit apprehensive as to whether the dishes should be rewashed to remove the soap. It is all right. The detergent is edible, anyway, and it will drip-dry. This Norwegian habit of dishwashing can be rather disconcerting at first, but when you have accepted that it is a norm, you can relax. After all, the hot water used to wash the dishes would have erased any dirt and destroyed germs lingering in the water.

## DOGS AND OTHER ANIMALS

You have relocated from your last posting or home, lock, stock, and barrel. This sometimes means dogs or cats. One quick word about bringing pets into Norway: quarantine.

Norway has very strict quarantine rules. If you have a favourite pet you cannot bear to leave behind, check with the immigration authorities or the Norwegian embassy in your country first. Both can clarify the matter for you. The fear of rabies is quite real in Norway. Because part of the country is agricultural land, Norway is very sensitive to imported plant and animal diseases. Hence, all pets must be quarantined on arrival in Norway, for at least six months, and absolutely no plants are allowed through customs.

There have been instances where tourists visiting Norway from other parts of Europe were not aware of the quarantine law and were unpleasantly shocked when they arrived, only to be told they could not bring their pets in. When one Spanish woman was told, in no uncertain terms, that her dog could not be brought into Norway, she opted not to visit the country. She loved her dog too much to be separated from it – however temporarily.

## TACKLING THE COMMUNICATION PROBLEM

The official language of communication is Norwegian. This is not unexpected, in view of the fact that 4 million of its total population of 4.3 million are Norwegian. There are deviations from the norm: up north, Samisk is the official language of the Sami inhabitants.

Many Norwegians, with the exception of those now in their 60s and older, can speak English quite fluently. But if you want to explore philosophy or deeper matters in English with a Norwegian, you might have to repeat yourself a few times.

Norwegian children know a smattering of English and German because these are the two main foreign languages taught in school. French is also a popular foreign language taught in secondary schools. Thus, when you are shopping, you discover to your great satisfaction that the sales assistants can speak English. But your best bet, when getting around in Norway, and especially if you intend to stay in Norway for a long period, is to learn the Norwegian language.

Learning Norwegian will open many doors to Norwegians and their institutions, and even perhaps to some gainful employment. Language learning is a means of acculturation and leads to a more effective acclimatisation process.

93

You can learn Norwegian informally in an interesting and enjoyable way. Read comics in Norwegian. Perhaps you think you are past the age: what will your children think? Probably that their parents are becoming more fun. It's much cheaper to share comics. Start with the recommended classics: *The Phantom* (Fantomet) based in South Africa – very romantic and exciting; *Donald Duck* is international; and *Smørbukk* is typically Norwegian fare. Have a pocket Norwegian-English dictionary by your side; a Norwegian acquaintance who can double up as a walking dictionary could be useful.

## Learning the Norwegian Language

The Norwegian language is closely related to the other Scandinavian languages and, to a lesser degree, to English, Dutch, and German. There are two official languages, *bokmål* and *nynorsk*, with equal status in official use and in schools. The Norwegian alphabet contains 29 letters, three of which are not found in the English alphabet. They are æ, ø, and å.

In the 14th century, succession to the Norwegian throne passed to the royal house of Denmark, and from 1397 till 1814, the two countries were in a union. Denmark was on the 'wrong' side in the Napoleonic Wars and 'lost' Norway to Sweden. From 1814 to 1905, Norway was in a union with Sweden. The focus of Norwegian administration and culture during the union lay in Copenhagen. The languages started to merge as a result of 400 years of largely Danish administration. (However, in Iceland, a country founded and settled by Norwegians around the year 1000, and which followed Norway into the union, early Norwegian languages continued to be spoken.)

Then in 1814 came political independence and the realisation that this so-called 'Norwegian' language was really Danish. Patriots rallied to the call for a true Norwegian language and denounced the use of Danish as a disgrace and a reminder of the inferior position of Norway in the union with Denmark. Agitation arose around 1835, headed by the great poet Henrik Wergeland (1808–45), to make the language more Norwegian. Since that time, the problem of which language to use has been one of the burning issues in the literary and political life of Norway.

In the cities, particularly Oslo, the educated middle-class speak a Norwegian that is based in part on written Danish, but with so many Norwegian elements that no Dane would recognise it as his own. This is *riksmål* or *bokmål*, the language with the greatest social and cultural prestige in Norway, the language of Wergeland, Bjørnstjerne Bjørnson, and Henrik Ibsen. By means of three successive spelling reforms – in 1907, 1917, and 1938 – its written form has been made to agree very closely with its spoken form. Because of its origin, it is often referred to as Dano-Norwegian.

However, many Norwegians do not feel comfortable with *bokmål*. Outside the cities, most Norwegians have continued to speak dialects not based upon Danish, but lineally descended from the Norwegian speech of ancient times. This influence is marked in the lower-class speech of the cities, which contains more Norwegian elements (feminine endings, for instance) than upper-class speech. Further into the countryside, the dialects grow more and more characteristically Norwegian, with less and less Danish admixture.

In some of the remote valleys of central and western Norway dialects were discovered that seemed to have the authentic native quality missing in the country's standard language. Ivar Åsen (1813–96), a linguistic genius, conceived the idea that if the most 'genuine' native dialects (those most like Old Norse) were studied, a form of Norwegian could be created, equivalent to what the national language would have been had Norway never been united with Denmark. Åsen followed his idea through and, in 1853, published his first specimen of this new language. He called it *landsmål*, a name by which it is still often known (although *nynorsk* is now the official name). In English, *landsmål* is called New Norse.

Depending on where in Norway you decide to stay, you will find yourself speaking a version of Norwegian that is either *bokmål* or *nynorsk*. Officially, in the public and educational sectors, both forms of Norwegian are accepted. Students taking examinations can answer questions in either type of Norwegian.

For more on language instruction and help in communication, see Chapter 5.

## Dates and Numbers in Norway

The system of writing dates and numbers should be memorised.

*Dates:*    Day, month, year: for example, 24.05.94 or 24 May 1994.

*Numbers:*  Periods denote thousands; commas denote decimals. For example, NOK 2.000,70 means two thousand Norwegian crowns and 70 øre. Instead of writing 27.4%, write 27,4%.

## GET BUSY!

Once you possess a certain competence in the Norwegian language, you can do several exciting things. This section is devoted to foreign women in Norway who find time on their hands.

Several organisations exist that you can join to get to know the Norwegians. One is the local women's group, known as the *Kvinnegruppe*. Another option, usually if you are a mother and a housewife, is to join the Housewives' Organisation or *Husmorlag*. Yet another is to enrol in an evening course at the local Extra-Mural Studies Department or *Friundervisningen*. Better still, you could even teach a course at *Friundervisningen*, perhaps a language or a cooking course! This is a great way to socialise informally.

There are also numerous choir, music, and keep-fit groups. If you are interested in politics, you may join a political party group.

## Join a Women's Group

The *Kvinnegruppe* is a gathering of mostly professional women interested in discussing women's issues and current literature. Women in such a group are usually in their mid-20s to mid-40s. While many are career women, artists, or teachers, there may also be university students or graduates. Women's groups like these spring up all over the locality, in different neighbourhoods or districts. You might like to join the group that meets every Tuesday or the group that meets at Inger's house down the road. Or you might have a good friend who goes to Eva's house on the other side of the river – the women there seem to share the same interests as you and you are comfortable in their company.

The women in a *Kvinnegruppe* are not liberal feminists, but it is inevitable, given the milieu they work or function in, for example a municipal office or a school, that they are interested in politics and debate. They tend to be more theoretical in context in the sense that they enjoy discussions on movies, current topics of interest, the working conditions of women, and their personal goals and problems. The group is usually discursive, somewhat academic in nature, and not very action-oriented. But it is great for interaction, a good cup of coffee in the evening with congenial and amusing company, and unwinding after a day at home or in the office. It is also a good grapevine (though gossiping is not the group's espoused intention).

An advantage of joining the *Kvinnegruppe* in your district is that you get to know the women neighbours better and can share in some social activities outside group meetings later. You can start batik painting sessions or exchange cake-making banter at each other's homes. Though, with the Norwegian woman's busy work schedule and domestic routine, she often finds that she has to juggle her time between work and home and friends. This might be an excuse you will hear again and again – as your Norwegian friend laments the shortness of hours in her day.

## *Join the Housewives' Organisation* – Husmorlag

You will be impressed by this great assembly of women in the *Husmorlag*. Members have a distinct prowess in the art of knitting – they knit apparently without even looking at their stitches, while chatting over cups of coffee or discussing the latest charity project.

If you think you have landed in the midst of a sewing circle, you will soon learn that appearances can be deceptive. The *Husmorlag* is a club that is part of a bigger organisation with affiliates in every town and city in Norway. In fact, it has a permanent representative in the Norwegian Parliament who lobbies for significant issues to help improve the lot of housewives, children, and families in Norway.

The *Husmorlag* is committed to social change as reflected in legislation of acts pertaining to the welfare of families. It has a say in television censorship and the discussion of the school curriculum. It organises charity bazaars, on the local level, to raise funds for a cause – a much-needed wheelchair for little handicapped Siri, for example. It runs self-improvement seminars on teaching women to make oral presentations in public, on debating and negotiation skills, and on awareness of women's roles in society. Every year, all the members of district affiliations meet at the annual get-together of the club, usually in the different municipal centres, where they discuss their recent activities, their budget, and the agenda for the coming year, and evaluate their aims and objectives.

All members are volunteers. Some of them are in their 60s and experts at knitting woollen socks with not two, but four knitting needles. Others are young housewives who want to do something useful with their time. It is a happy mix.

You can find your niche somewhere among those knitting and crotchet needles, lucky draw tickets, campaigns for prizes for the bazaars, etc. Whatever the activity, you will enjoy yourself. The group usually meets in some member's house, at the church hall, or in the local coffee-house. You'll have good coffee with sandwiches or homemade specialities like waffles with goat cheese. The company is pleasant and the pace very relaxing, especially in winter when the group meeting takes on a special cosiness indoors.

How do you join? You get recruited by your Norwegian neighbour or friend, or ask to join. The group always welcomes new members. The more, the merrier.

*Active and interested participants of all ages at a county* Husmorlag *workshop where they explore women's issues and brainstorm ideas.*

## *Start an Evening Class*

Another way to meet the locals is to offer your services as a part-time teacher with the Norwegian education department's Extra-Mural Services Centre (*Friundervisningen*). You know your own skills; show them off. Use them to earn some money and make new friends, and in the process share your culture with the Norwegians.

Culture shock is not a one-way process. It is not only the incoming foreigner who gets disoriented when she enters Norway. The Norwegian who suddenly finds an African, an Asian, or an American on her doorstep also experiences culture shock and needs time and help to absorb it all and learn to accept and adapt.

If you call the local education department, you can find out more about the kinds of courses the department is interested in organising. You will then have a better idea of how you can fit into the system.

## *Conduct a Language Course*

Some of the more popular courses seem to be English or Spanish language and cooking. Many Norwegians are fond of improving their language skills – and they include washing ladies, the women who wash schools and offices after work. Do not be surprised that these women know not a word of English, not even the English alphabet, when they join you. Sign language and expressive hand and facial gestures go a long way in initial exchange. You will find real satisfaction in your teaching skills and the determination of your students when they graduate at the end of one year of classes with you, knowing how to conduct a simple conversation in English.

When teaching English to Norwegian learners, be prepared to do some translation; it is absolutely necessary in the early part of your teaching. Sometimes a little translation goes a long way in getting your point across effectively. Always make sure you are prepared for your lessons. Norwegians are astute observers of lazy teachers who do not deliver. They can be quite critical of teaching methods and efficiency. So protect yourself and your professionalism by being prepared for class.

Self-improvement courses are normally held in spring and autumn, but never in summer. In summer, Norwegians are too busy with their gardens, or their summer home projects, or rest and recreation, to bother to attend courses at the local school classroom or kitchen. Schools are the usual venues of these courses because they are conducted under the auspices of the local education department in the district.

Books for language courses are provided by the department. Winter brings a marketing blitz on the television network about approaching language courses whose oral components are telecast. There is excellent coordination between the media and the national, private, or correspondence schools. To supplement the textbooks, stations televise the audio-visual text. This is not only a very good way for Norwegians and other interested residents in the country to improve their skills in languages; language learning is a useful hobby in the winter, which can be long and dreary if not utilised well.

## Start a Cooking Class

Are you kidding? you ask. You have never taught people how to cook before, and have only cooked for your family. Sure, you like cooking, but will people like what you teach them to cook? Let me tell you that Norwegians appreciate a taste of foreign cuisine.

Among Asian cuisines, Chinese fried rice and spring rolls are regular favourites. Sweet and sour dishes have also been popularised by the many Hong Kong restaurants flourishing in the big cities in Norway. Indian meat cutlets and *dhal* (lentil) curry are well appreciated. Norwegians would not be averse to learning to cook these dishes in their own kitchens.

Some Norwegians are really quite adventurous in their culinary tastes. Spaghetti and pizza are on the plates of most Norwegian families at least once a month. If you know how, you could teach Norwegians more pasta dishes with more tantalising sauces. They love Mediterranean and Continental cuisines.

Don't be afraid to use the short cuts if you lack experience in some areas. If you have never made spring roll skin before, for example, don't try. You may be game but you don't have to wallow around in dough up to your elbows to create your own spring roll skin. It can be bought from foreign-owned (Vietnamese or Hong Kong) provision stores in most large towns.

You may have to create your own recipes. Improvise. Unless it tastes really horrible, Norwegians will be intrigued. Of course, you should test your own concoctions. Experiment with yourself – and then turn yourself out on the whole wide world in Norway! If you do not know how to write adequately in Norwegian, ask a friend to translate. Or else subscribe to the local cooking magazines and read their recipes in Norwegian. Very soon, you will know how to say *sauté*, *knead*, and all kinds of useful culinary verbs in Norwegian.

## Winter Strategy for Class Interaction

In winter, the usual period for the lessons, you can always suggest at the beginning of class that you and the students take turns to bring hot coffee and tea, as well as some snacks, be it cookies, cake, or waffles. Norwegians seldom eat sandwiches at that time, which is normally after dinner, from about 6 p.m. to 8 p.m. This is a wonderful way for the class to take a break and relax, and get to know each other personally.

At the end of a term, if you like, you can invite the class to your house for an end-of-term party. Norwegians love parties and they also reciprocate, especially if they decide they like you. Do not feel shy about saying it is only a tea gathering and not dinner. Norwegian acquaintances do not expect to be invited to dinner, not unless their host is wealthy or extravagant. Tea with hot snacks or even just cakes is fine. Norwegians are unpretentious in their expectations. The fact that you took the trouble to invite them to your house when you didn't need to will register and be remembered by some. Your simple gesture will plant the seed of friendship somewhere in that crowd.

## Enrol in a Home Study Group

Norway enjoys a proliferation of self-study self-improvement courses offered by institutions such as NF (*Norsk Friundervisning*) or NKS (*Norsk Korrespondanse Skole* – Norwegian Correspondence School). A good means of interaction is to start or join a study group on Norwegian literature, for example, or Norwegian desserts. Brochures can be obtained from a library display unit or by writing to the institutions directly. Find out more about such courses, which are popular as a way to get together socially and have a great deal of fun, learning together.

Home study groups are usually the result of enrolling in a distance education programme. Education by correspondence has for many years played an important role in Norway. An Act concerning correspondence schools, passed in 1948, ensures that all courses offered by such schools are approved and the schools' activities supervised by the national authorities. About 22 correspondence schools offer some 1,000 courses, the majority being vocational or leading to formal qualifications. Several of the schools are now cooperating with higher educational institutions in setting up courses, particularly in subjects such as media knowledge, economics, and administration.

The Norwegian State Institute for Distance Education was set up in 1977 and is primarily engaged in distance programmes for adult education, based on radio, television, or video and text material.

## *Join the Local Library*

The library is a very good source for your learning endeavours. You will be able to find English, German, and French literature in the library, depending on how big it is. There used to be a travelling library that made the rounds of towns without their own library building. This was to encourage Norwegians to cultivate the reading habit.

Today, all Norwegians are literate. Their favourite reading materials are the daily newspapers, special interest journals or magazines, to which many of them subscribe, be they professional or recreational, and fiction. Books are reasonably priced in Norway, and there are also mail order book clubs you can join. If you do not want to spend a great deal of money buying literature in Norway, pay periodic visits to your local library, a rich mine of resources.

The library sometimes organises reading groups or book clubs where participating members read and discuss their book of the month or argue over the relative merits of the latest bestseller. The library is also where the latest government or municipal gazette is displayed for public perusal and criticism before it is passed as law. Sometimes the library is where intellectuals, housewives, politicians, and office workers meet to thresh out the merits and disadvantages of the latest paper on, for instance, reducing the number of kindergarten places in the district and what this means in practice. On selected evenings, it is a forum for the exchange of views.

If you have a pet project to advertise, ask the librarian for permission to display it on the entrance doors that visitors will have to pass through. As the library is usually located in a place of high visibility, your poster will get the attention it deserves.

## *Take Part in Your Children's School Activities*

If you have children, your access to interaction with Norwegians is guaranteed. Norwegians are very family-oriented. School is recognised as an important part of Norwegian children's life as they spend at least half the day in school. Parent-teacher associations are part and parcel of every school in Norway, but just how active and effective these associations are depends on the leadership and initiative shown.

Schools organise visits for parents to take part in workshop-style activities just prior to Christmas to make decorations and watch a Christmas pageant or show put on by the students. They may also have regular meet-the-teacher sessions for parents. Teacher-parent consultation is perceived as a part of the learning process for both parties as they attempt to understand the child in his or her totality, at school and at home. Parents can also volunteer for the school's reading programme for learners of English or the mother tongue.

It is almost customary for every class to elect a representative from among the parents to be class spokesman for the parents. The representative can decide to hold regular monthly parents' sessions to update other parents on latest developments at school. These sessions are a great opportunity for parents to discuss the problems they have with their children and offer mutual solace or advice.

These groups could function as a parents' outlet for voicing their concern that their Elin is saying her best friend Guro is allowed to stay up to watch the late-night movie every Thursday: is this true? Elin wants to follow suit, but her parents are worried. Such discussions can be confrontational, but they can also be therapeutic and helpful.

If you are a foreigner suffering from culture shock in bringing up your children in the Norwegian environment, parents' group meetings can clarify issues and help resolve other issues as well. But you must be daring and diplomatic enough to get some local support, before you start the ball rolling in this direction.

## OTHER SURVIVAL STRATEGIES

### Learn to Bake!

A fine way to make friends and introduce yourself to the neighbours is to do the rounds with a cake or an exciting-looking loaf of bread.

It may take you months to produce a beautiful cake that can stand upright without collapsing. But do it. Don't wait for perfection; that moment may never come in this lifetime. Do your best, and when you think your creation is good enough to give away, do just that. Norwegians are not picky people who must have the best of Maxim's or the most voluptuous cake imaginable before they pronounce that you pass whatever test you set yourself. Most Norwegian women can bake so it is no big deal. But they will appreciate your gesture of friendship, even if your bread is kind of hard and the cake looks … interesting.

## *Join a Club*

New arrivals usually feel somewhat lost and disoriented. The people speak a different language and many things seem alien. You long for some familiar signs, to eat familiar food, see familiar faces. What you should do then is join a club.

In the cities, it is easy to check out the associations affiliated to your own culture. Your embassy is a good starting point. If you are American, you will find that there is an American club you can join. It could be a formal group with its own clubhouse or a group of Americans who meet regularly somewhere and do things together. You can get a contact telephone number and make your first move, which could be the start of some lasting relationships that will give you support during your stay in Norway.

Norway abounds in group cultures. There are lots of clubs to join – athletics, rifle-shooting (which happens to be very popular in Norway), and football are just a few sports clubs. There are also clubs for recreation, such as wine appreciation clubs and the evergreen bridge club (bridge is well-liked in Norway).

If you are single and lonely, you can learn to read the advertisements in the local dailies as well as some other newspapers. You will be amazed at the explicit statements of longing and desire for companionship. Most of these advertisements are in the classified section and carry with them names, ages, and post office box numbers where you can address your enquiries. In the cities, there are the usual cafeterias and singles bars where you can hang out, if you wish.

## SIGNALS FROM THE GROUND

How do you know you have been accepted by Norwegians?

You have lived in Norway for a few months, a year, several years. How will you know when they have welcomed you into their midst and call you one of their own? Some people say that no matter how long you live in Norway, if you are a foreigner, you can never be one of them. You are distinctive in your shape, size, colour, and values.

You have your own cultural identity. That is fine; acculturation does not mean giving up your old values totally and adopting new ones easily overnight. There is always exchange and sharing, never a one-sided exclusiveness.

Nevertheless, it would be good to know the signs of acceptance – they boost your morale and make you feel all your efforts to adapt have not been made in vain.

You will know you have become a friend to a Norwegian when he or she has you dropping over for informal chats over coffee or wine in the evening. There is no need to wait to be invited over, though it is always thoughtful to check if your visit comes at a suitable time and does not inconvenience your friend. You will know when to pop over when your friend tells you that you are welcome anytime and means it. Norwegians usually do not say things they do not mean. This open invitation is such an opportunity for social interaction and personal sharing, especially in winter when the nights are long and dark. Sitting in a warm living room, enjoying apple cake with coffee, or sipping wine in between nibbles of cheese in cosy comfort is something not to be missed.

You will know when your Norwegian friend starts confiding in you about problems at work or at home. They may be problems with an adolescent child in the family – dating, peer group pressure, things like that. Or your friend starts reminiscing about the old courting days or family. Then you know he or she is opening up to you. It takes time for a Norwegian to become emotionally intimate with anyone, and the notion of the person allowing his or her private life to be open to you is a telling gesture of acceptance.

You will know when you and your Norwegian girlfriend share your mutual loneliness in the depths of winter, when both of you are feeling miserable and alone. Yes, it is not only you who experiences all that awful rain and sludge and darkness outside, and feel a corresponding darkness within. Norwegians feel this loneliness too. But if you ask them why they do not open up their homes and their hearts in winter, they will say they are Norwegians and have grown up with these feelings and should be used to managing them. It all has to do with the amount of light we get in winter. Something in our bodies reacts to the light or darkness and triggers off a chemical reaction that sets us off on a spiral of depression.

The first winter in Norway is exciting. You see and taste snow for the first time, and you learn to ski. Everything outside is white and beautiful. Then the second winter comes and it seems too long and dreary. You mope around the house and hope to be invited to Norwegian homes. No one invites you, and you begin to despair. Norwegians seem to be like hibernating animals in winter – they close their doors to the outside. Taking a risk, you visit your neighbour and find, to your surprise, that she feels as miserable as you. At one point, you are so lonely you go over to your neighbour's and you cry. And then she tells you it's all right, she cries too in winter. You know then that she is sharing herself with you.

## *KEEPING TIME IN NORWAY*

Norwegians keep local time, which is Greenwich Mean Time plus one hour. In the period from 28 March to 29 September, Norway uses summer time (daylight saving time), which is the same as Greenwich Mean Time. As a comparison, United States Eastern Standard Time is Greenwich Mean Time minus five hours.

Norwegians' normal working time is 37.5 hours per week; working hours vary, depending on the nature of business. The Workers' Protection Act contains regulations concerning the conditions of work and stipulates the maximum working hours: 9 hours per day, 40 hours per week. In principle, all night work is prohibited, including work on Sundays and public holidays.

Normal office hours are from 8 a.m. to 4 p.m., but in summer, office workers stop work at 3 p.m. Summer is a time for enjoying the sun as far as possible and all Norwegians should be given the right to stretch out their summer time.

What this means in practice is that there is a lot of time for leisure and family activities. This reinforces the notion that Norwegians know how to balance their work and play. In workaholic societies, having the luxury of time to call one's own is a rarity. But in Norway, it is part of the lifestyle.

# REST AND RECREATION

In this section, you may discover an inclination for activities that may give you hours of leisure enjoyment.

## Fishing

Norway is renowned for its salmon and trout. Going out in a small boat in a fjord, equipped with fishing tackle, a companion, and lots of enthusiasm is one experience the adventurous should not ignore. An even more exciting experience is river trout fishing. Fishing enthusiasts from as far away as Japan, the United States of America, England, and Germany have come to fish here.

Angling with rod and handline for saltwater fish in the sea is free of charge for everyone. But it is a different matter when you want to catch something in inland waters.

### Get a Fishing Licence

State and regional regulations monitor inland fishing. You have to be aware of these rules governing fishing rights before you start angling in Norway. About two-thirds of all land in Norway is privately owned. Fishing rights in Norwegian watercourses usually belong to the landowner, a rule that applies regardless of whether the watercourse is privately, commonly, or government-owned.

In order to fish, a fishing licence or the landowner's permission is required. The licence may be purchased in the fishing locality from the landowner, at sporting goods dealers, tourist information offices, and campsites. Lists of fishing areas covered by different licences are available for many counties and municipalities. Information on

109

where, how, and when to fish is often provided on the back of the licence. Several types of fishing licences exist, with validity varying from one day, two days, or one week, to an entire season.

Far fewer restrictions are imposed on inland fishing than for salmon fishing. Inland fishing is generally permitted throughout the year, with any kind of tackle not prohibited by law. What is important to remember is that the use of live fish as bait is prohibited. This precaution is enforced to prevent the introduction of new species from one watercourse to another – a factor that may interrupt the effective management of an environment conducive to the protection of the fish population in Norway. For example, several trout lakes in Norway have been ruined by fishermen using live minnows as bait.

*Fishing Rights for Children*
If you have children below 16 years old, they can participate in inland fishing with a rod and handline free of charge from 1 January to 20 August. In watercourses where licences are required, children should carry a licence obtained free of charge. In areas where fishing licences are not required, landowner permission is not necessary. The regulation on free fishing for children does not apply in artificial fishing ponds, and the county governor's environmental department reserves the right to restrict fishing in particular lakes.

*Observe the Fishing Rules*
Fish diseases represent a serious threat to fishery resources, thus all anglers must observe certain fishing guidelines, among which are recommendations on cleaning fish, fish tackles, and what to do when you catch diseased fish. Contact the authorities for the list of rules.

## Rights of Passage on Uncultivated Earth
Norway does not proclaim boundaries that exclude people from enjoying the beautiful landscape and scenery. This liberty is recognised as 'the right of passage on uncultivated earth'. Many of us are

used to the idea of declaring our rights to our own property by erecting fences to keep trespassers out. Sometimes, the property might not be developed land but is mainly grassland or mountainous terrain. In Norway, there is a respect for private property, but at the same time, there is a belief that all things natural should be enjoyed by as many people as possible as long as they do not deface or vandalise the property. Nature is made for everyone.

As such, there is an unlegislated law in Norway, known as the right of passage. Going on a fishing trip, for instance, might necessitate walking on foot in areas that are not cultivated, are in fact part of the wild. The right of passage includes picnicking, camping, and setting up a tent on uncultivated land. All areas except cultivated earth (such as fields, meadows, and gardens), cultivated pasturage (such as hayfields and forest planting areas), planted areas, home sites, farm-yards, and associated buildings are regarded as outfields or *utmark*, and are open for free passage. You may walk about, unmolested and unaccosted. You may pick mushrooms and berries in such areas.

This public right of access is part of the Norwegian cultural heritage. It has been confirmed in the Norwegian Outdoor Recreation Act, which aims, among other things, to clarify the relation between the use of land for recreation on the one hand and for commercial purposes on the other. In the Outdoor Recreation Act, the terms 'cultivated land' and 'uncultivated land' are used to define and delimit the right of access. It confers the right to hike and ski, and cross cultivated land in winter (when the ground is frozen or covered with snow); to use a canoe or kayak, rowing boat or sailboat on lakes and rivers (as well as frozen watercourses); to rest, picnic, put up tents, spend the night, cycle, and ride a horse along paths and roads across uncultivated land; to swim in the sea, lakes, and rivers, to go by boat, moor, and go ashore on uncultivated land along the coast.

The public right of access also imposes obligations. The Outdoor Recreation Act requires all country-goers to behave considerately and with care. You must not damage the natural environment, and show

*A day's outing, with backpack and packed sandwiches, then stopping to rest by a rippling brook, seems a good idea. The right of passage gives one the right to enjoy the outdoors, but carries with it an obligation to keep the environment clean.*

consideration for commercial interests as well as for other country-goers. There should be no unnecessary disturbance of landowners or other users of nature. These general rules imply that you may not:

- trample fields and meadows;
- walk about in newly planted forest not covered by snow (from the time the trees are planted until they are knee-high);
- break off, cut, or in any way damage trees and other plants;
- disturb animals and birds, including their nests and their young; and
- damage fences.

Other rules to observe when out in the open are:

- You must not camp within 150 metres of a house or cabin. Your tent may not remain at the same location for more than two days without the landowner's permission. The other nature-users' right to privacy should be respected.

- You are allowed to pick berries in areas regarded as *utmark*, but this does not include cloudberry-picking in Nordland, Troms, and Finnmark. This is because some people in these areas gather cloudberries for income and the landowners have the right to the cloudberries.
- Lighting a campfire is prohibited from 15 April to 15 September, except in the mountainous areas above the treeline. This is to safeguard against forest fires in summertime.
- If you have dogs walking with you, keep them on a leash at all times from 1 April to 20 August, and at other times in the vicinity of grazing animals.
- You must keep the environment clean. If there are no rubbish bins for disposal of waste, take your own trash away with you.

## Using a Boat

On lakes and fjords, rowboats and boats without engines are permitted almost everywhere. You can only use the motorboat in the sea and in lakes greater than 2 square kilometres. Drivers must be over 16 years old when driving boats with engines exceeding 10 horsepower or at speeds exceeding 10 knots. A driving licence is not required for boats with weights less than 25 tonnes.

## Mountain Hikes and Climbing

Norway has extensive mountain trails for hiking and walking. In fact, there are marked trails as long as the distance from Oslo to Tokyo. Along the route are special cabins with self-service or larger lodges. You can easily drive to these places. This system functions from June to September and during Easter (for cross-country skiing).

During the summer, there is sometimes an orienteering route for interested participants. Families who like walking and exploring the countryside can buy specially-designed packs that give the routes and present the challenges. These orienteering tours are really fun for family outings, and you can take your own time to complete the course. The duration of the orienteering activity is several months and the packs can be purchased from petrol stations or sports shops. There is no competition but the sense of self-fulfilment that comes from enjoying an exciting outdoor activity is reward enough.

### Glacier Walking

In Norway, you can do all sorts of unusual activities you have never indulged in before. Glacier walking is one adventure. Norwegian glaciers are tantalising, and seeing this expanse of packed ice induces a wanderlust to play intrepid explorer. Before you wander off to explore a mountain or glacier on your own, however, it is important to remember that these activities need some special prior knowledge. Courses are offered at several places, especially for glacier walking. You can enrol for them and learn about the proper technique and equipment for enjoyable and safe glacier walking.

When you go glacier walking, you will usually have a guide. You will find it is like entering a wonderful subterranean world of light, splendour, and beauty. A glacier is colourless or white, but has shades of blue and green, depending on the amount of oxygen in the ice. And always remember that a glacier can move. A moving glacier is a danger, so observe all warning signs and notices.

## Gardening in Oslo

In the suburbs of Oslo is a small community of home gardeners with little plots of land and little houses that stand as a reminder of the urban status of Oslo. The Norwegian Association of Home Gardeners honours a tradition established for over half a century, namely communing with the soil.

In Oslo, an area is specially set aside for people who want to do part-time gardening. Many of them are older people who have bought these plots and return in the summer to indulge in their hobby. The houses are thus only partially occupied the whole year round. It is only a little piece of land, but the principle behind it is a noteworthy acknowledgement that a Norwegian needs to keep in touch with the earth.

It is a fact that many Norwegians love to work in their gardens in the summer. They plant crocuses and tulip buds in the autumn and wait for them to flower in the summer. They weed their garden, turn the soil, and generally perceive their cultivated plot as a reflection of themselves and an extension of the internal spaces within the house. A sloppy garden tells observers that the owner is sloppy and does not bother with the proper tending of the soil.

The garden is sometimes brought indoors – in the form of little potted plants or herbs for the kitchen window-sill. Norwegians love to see green in the home. It brings a bit of spring and summer into a house. And when it is cold and dark outside, the plants inside bring warmth and cheer.

# Chapter Four

# BREAD, POTATO, AND AQUAVIT

While walking along the main street in town, you suddenly see hordes of Norwegians converging on a little shop in the middle of a block. There is excitement and impatience, and you are naturally interested in this rare public display of emotion. What is happening here?

It is probably the eve of a public holiday, and the Norwegians are all rushing to stock up their wine larders. The shop you see is the Norwegian *vinmonopol* (literally 'wine monopoly'), a name every Norwegian knows. The Monopol is the officially designated outlet for the sale of whisky and other liquors and wines. It is impossible to buy these drinks anywhere else in Norway, hence the slightly unusual degree of passion exhibited in the usually calm and composed Norwegian.

Norway has an interesting policy regarding the sale and distribution of alcohol and the development of Norwegian drinking habits. In the mid-19th century, the unrestricted production of whisky resulted in severe social problems. A strong temperance movement emerged, which led to the implementation of prohibition against fortified wine and whisky in 1916. These restrictions were rescinded in 1927, but thereafter all sales of wine and spirits had to go through a monopoly, and the number of sales outlets and liquor licences was restricted. By the mid-1980s, the policy was liberalised and now you can find Monopol outlets at supermarkets, a more convenient location.

Norwegians who travel abroad will take advantage of their liquor and wine quota to purchase their supply of spirits at the airport before returning home. Norwegians who live far from towns will make a special effort to visit the Monopol outlet when they go to the city. When you visit a Norwegian home, know that a bottle of liquor or wine will be welcomed and accepted with great appreciation.

## NORWEGIAN BEER

Because the prices of beer and wine at the Monopol are not low, some more enterprising and adventurous Norwegians have taken to making their own wines at home. If you are invited to a Norwegian home and brought down to the cellar to see their home wine-making apparatus, you will be surprised at the ingenuity of Norwegians in preparing their own drink all the way. Homemade beer or wine can be good or not so good. Your Norwegian hosts will make the pronouncement and you can trust their judgement.

Beer is a typical Nordic drink, and in summer particularly, outdoor restaurants sell a lot of beer. One popular beer is *pils*, which has about 4–5% alcohol. *Pils* is quite pleasant and has a refreshing flavour; somehow, it tastes wonderfully good in summer. Women are also fond of their occasional pint of *pils*.

Beer is always best when it is newly tapped, and it should not be stored longer than three months. It is served in a glass or tankard, depending on the occasion. If you are serving beer to Norwegian guests, you should know that weak beer is served colder than beer with a higher alcohol content.

Beer drinking is part of the Norwegian cultural history. Both in Viking times and during the Middle Ages, the beer bowl was the centre of attraction. To celebrate a birth, wedding, or funeral, beer was drunk. Beer had to be served to make an agreement legally binding. A law of the time, called the Gulating law, stated that nobody should be declared incompetent so long as he had his senses, could ride a horse, and drink beer. The Norwegian traffic police today would have something else to say on the subject!

## *POTATO WHISKY OR* AQUAVIT – *IT'S LETHAL!*

If you are at a party and your Norwegian host invites you to drink *aquavit*, be warned. 'What is *aquavit*?' you ask. Your host tells you it is potato whisky. 'How interesting,' you say, as you look at the glass of innocuous white water in your hand. *Is it strong?* you wonder. Dismissing the idea – how can whisky made from potatoes be strong? – you take a big gulp. And your eyes pop out of your head and your throat is on fire. You don't know what has hit you. Potatoes? Unbelievable.

Unbelievable, but true.

*Aquavit* is the Scandinavian contribution to the world's gallery of unforgettable liquors. First sold as medicine in the 16th century, *aquavit* is a flavoured whisky containing caraway as an essential ingredient. Other herbs and spices used in the production of *aquavit* include anise, fennel, coriander, star anise, and bitter orange peel. Small amounts of Oloroso sherry, sugar, and salt are also added to combine into the well-rounded, developed taste. The name *aquavit* is derived in 1531 from a whisky created by Eske Bille and sent to the archbishop, Olav Engelbrektsson, as Aqua Vitæ – a cure for all ills.

Today, *aquavit* is made from neutral potato spirits. Tone Solberg tells us, in *The Norwegian Kitchen*, just what goes into *aquavit* production. The filtered alcohol is blended with distillates to a strength of 60%, and the mixture is aged for three to five years in 500 litre oak barrels, which previously were used in sherry production. The spices and herbs mix and merge, together with the oxygen absorbed through the pores of the barrel and the bunghole, to give a distinctive texture.

The first Norwegian whisky was made with grain, and people used their ingenuity to come up with all kinds of contraptions to distil it at home. Home distilling was forbidden from 1756 to 1816 to ensure the availability of grain for planting and to protect Danish breweries, but moonshine continued to be produced in every town and settlement. By the time controls were tightened in 1845, the production and consumption of spirits had gone completely out of control. It was estimated that in 1827, there were 11,000 distillation apparatuses in use in Norway, and drunkenness had become a major social problem. In 1857, only 450 stills were left, a reduction due not only to prohibition but also to the replacement of grain by the potato as the basic component. Making spirits from potatoes requires more advanced equipment and a greater volume of production, and not many Norwegians found it easy to make at home.

One feature of Norwegian *aquavit* is that it is seldom consumed alone. *Aquavit* always accompanies food such as *lutefisk* (a special fish dish), lamb and cabbage, or dried meats. It is supposed to accompany a main course and should be served at room temperature.

Linje (Line) Aquavit is well-known in Norway and Europe. Its name hints of its special nature. It is called Linje Aquavit or Linie Aquavit because the *aquavit* has passed over the equator or 'the line'. Years ago, sailing ships from Trøndelag used to transport Norwegian whisky to foreign countries. On some voyages, not all the whisky was sold or consumed, and what was left had to be brought back to Norway. Once in port, these bottles were sampled, and the tasters noticed that the long journey over the equator had given the whisky a completely new and wonderful aroma. From the 1850s, *aquavit* was aged on board, the oak vats sailing between Norway and Australia. That tradition has continued until the present time. The back label on each bottle notes the name of the ship used to transport the *aquavit*, where it has been, and how long it was en route.

## WINE MAKING AT HOME

Norway is too far north for the successful cultivation of grapes on a large scale. Apart from a certain amount of industrial production of fruit wines and vermouth, wine is imported. If you like to drink wine, you might try to make your own at home, as some Norwegians do.

Making wine from fruit and berries is a popular hobby in Norway. The wine must be aged for at least a year, usually in a cool place like the cellar. Some people have turned to 'quick wines' where chemicals are used to shorten the fermentation process. But most Norwegians like things natural and are willing to wait for their wines to age. True fruit wines can be exquisitely light and refreshing.

What kinds of fruits and berries should you look for after you buy your wine-making kit? Choose red currants, apples, rhubarb, and blueberries. If patience is your strong point, you can pick kilos of golden dandelions in the spring to make an excellent aperitif wine.

## GLØGG

At Christmas, Norwegians enjoy a warm concoction of juice seasoned with raisins, ginger, cardamoms, and other spices. This drink, called *gløgg*, is served warm, with raisins and bits of almonds floating on top. It is a lovely fragrant drink that children and adults like.

Perhaps *gløgg* is a reminder of the ancient Viking drink, mead. When the Vikings feasted, they toasted with mead, which was regarded as a substantially strong drink that was better than beer. Old recipes indicate that mead was usually made from water, sugar, lemons, syrup, ginger, raisins, and yeast.

*A neighbourhood picnic in the garden, amidst the late-blooming dandelions which are golden in summer and beard-white fluff in late bloom. Dandelion wine is made from golden dandelion.*

## COFFEE – BLACK, PLEASE

Norwegians have embraced coffee-drinking with a vengeance. Coffee first came to Norway about 250 years ago, but it wasn't generally accepted until the 1870s. Its patrons were an elitist group because coffee was then both foreign and expensive. Today, Norwegians are among the world's biggest consumers of coffee per inhabitant. Coffee is the perfect accompaniment to meals where bread is consumed, and the cold climate makes drinking a cup of steaming hot coffee a particular pleasure.

If you are used to coffee with milk and sugar, you will be in for a rude shock in Norway. Norwegians shudder to think that some people could add milk or sugar to their coffee. Ever the purist, they take their coffee strong and black. Festive dinners usually round off with a cup of strong black coffee and a glass of cognac or liqueur.

121

## TEA – A NEW FASHION

Norwegians have never been great tea drinkers. In the 1970s, in the wake of the hippie movement and the new political left, young people started to drink tea. Today, there is a new trend among younger Norwegians who perceive tea-drinking as a healthier alternative to coffee. Earlier, tea was served only on formal occasions and also to the infirm. Norwegians favour Earl Grey and Chinese tea, as well as herbal tea. Ceylon tea has not caught on in Norway.

## MILK – THE DAILY DRINK

All Norwegians love milk, being born into a milk-drinking culture. When Norwegian children come home after school, they head for the refrigerator for a glass of cold fresh milk. At supper, Norwegian couples have their sandwiches with milk. At breakfast, Norwegian workers head off to a full day's work fuelled with bread and milk.

Various selections of milk – fullcream, halfcream, skimmed, extra-thin – suit a variety of tastes and diets. Combinations of milk with yogurt also exist. Milk is a Norwegian staple and, besides being drunk, is often used in cooking.

Norway has strict rules regarding cattle-rearing and the milk you drink is of the highest quality. Norwegian red cattle are a result of thorough and planned breeding. There is no gene manipulation, no controversial research methods. Hormones and growth-stimulating drugs are not allowed – directly or through the feed. Norway prohibits the use of antibiotics in cattle production as well.

All milk produced in Norway goes to central dairies owned by the milk producers or co-ops. These dairies are associated with the Norwegian Milk Producers' Organisation, which established Norwegian Dairies as a sales and marketing apparatus. Norwegian Dairies markets about 20 different varieties of milk, 70 different cheeses, cream, sour cream, ice cream, dessert puddings, and sauces. In addition to three kinds of butter, they also produce a margarine-butter blend.

## COCOA AND HOT CHOCOLATE

If you leave Norway without trying its cocoa and hot chocolate, you would have missed something special. These drinks are especially popular among children, but if you are on a long walk or ski expedition, there is nothing more delicious than drinking hot chocolate from a thermos flask up in the mountains.

Norwegian cocoa tastes so good that one is hardly surprised to learn that Norway boasts of a very famous chocolate factory, immortalised in Norwegian-American author Roald Dahl's book, *Charlie and the Chocolate Factory*. The factory in question is Freia and the chocolates it produces are heavenly.

## CHOCOLATES GALORE AND FREIA!

Mention Norwegian chocolate and the name Freia instantly comes to mind. Freia is a brand name that covers about 40% of Norwegian demand for chocolate and sugar products. With regard to chocolate, Freia holds an even stronger position. Every other bar of chocolate sold in Norway is made by Freia. At the turn of the 19th century, two-thirds of all chocolate and sugar products consumed in Norway were imported, and one-third was produced in Norway. Today, the situation has reversed: one-third is imported and two-thirds are produced nationally. Every Norwegian consumes, on average, eight kilos of chocolate annually. Half of this is produced by Freia.

Freia started in a small way in 1892 when its founder Johan Throne Holst bought a small chocolate factory in a backyard at Rodelokka in Oslo, together with his brother and brother-in-law. The company has expanded and developed but is still at Rodelokka. Freia is a Norwegian success story. Besides being a pioneer in technology by developing a factory laboratory, Freia recognised the importance of retail outlets and an extensive range of products. Perhaps one of the great selling points of Norwegian chocolate and Freia is the endorsement of the famous Norwegian explorer Roald Amundsen. He stated categorically after his return from his major South Pole expedition,

'Freia chocolate was one of our main sources of nourishment during the expedition.'

'Chocolate spells joy' is the slogan for all of Freia's chocolates, but each product has an identity of its own. Firkløver is the chocolate bar for breaks in a hectic day – it has little bits of almond for a crunchy flavour. KvikkLunsj is the chocolate to eat on a hike – it is a wafer biscuit liberally spread with luscious chocolate. Freia Milk Chocolate is known outside Norway as 'a little piece of Norway' – it is smooth and milky-rich in texture. If you are going to make it a long stay in Norway, you will be thankful to have discovered a lifetime passion in Norwegian chocolate.

Freia is not only associated with chocolate but with culture and art in Norway. Promoting the arts has become part of the company's profile, and Freia has publicly supported the arts in many ways. In the 1920s, the Freia Park was created to enhance the well-being of its employees. The result is one of Oslo's finest parks. Sculptures by a number of European artists can be found there. In central place is Gustav Vigeland's *Girl Riding a Bear*. (Gustav Vigeland is the national sculptor responsible for the fantastic sculptures in the Vigeland or Frognar Park in Oslo.) In 1922, Edvard Munch was invited to decorate Freia's three lunch rooms. Munch himself supervised the hanging of his paintings in the new Freia Hall after it was built. Opened in 1934, the hall has been diligently used for concerts by the Oslo Philharmonic Orchestra.

# PÅLEGG

The word *pålegg* is almost untranslatable in any other language. It is unique to the Norwegian vocabulary and means 'something to put on bread'. Open-face sandwiches are a popular meal in Norway. *Pålegg* is what goes on the top of these sandwiches. It could be ham, salami, egg, cheese, sardines, cucumber, tomato, liver paté, jam – any combination you like. Norwegians are very fond of having bread with *pålegg* as a meal or a snack.

*The Norwegian diet comprises a simple mix of milk, bread, cheese, and vegetables. Open sandwiches are the norm for lunch.*

## POTATOES, POTATOES...
## AARGH – POTATOES AGAIN!

The common potato is a much valued tuber in Norway. It is so much used in Norwegian kitchens that no Norwegian can conceive of a main meal without the ubiquitous potato. It is eaten boiled, baked, fried as chips, sliced and baked in a fricassee, served in soups... So be prepared when you are confronted with the potato in Norway – do not throw up your hands in despair and say you need rice, not potatoes;

125

you need pasta, not potatoes; you need greens, not potatoes. Potatoes are what they have more than enough of in Norway and potatoes are what you will get, so learn to enjoy them.

The potato was introduced to Europe in the 16th century and arrived in Norway in the 18th century. Apparently, government employees and the upper classes, almost out of curiosity, were the first to plant potatoes in their gardens. The clergy soon realised that the potato was an important resource and used their influential position to spread word of the benefits of this vegetable. Thus arose the phenomenon of the 'potato preachers'. Farmers were wooed and convinced, and the potato took root in Norwegian soil. There were no regrets, especially during the famine years from 1804 to 1814, when hunger forced people to grow potatoes for their own use.

Today, Norwegians who have gardens love to plant and harvest their own little crops of potatoes in autumn. Growing their own vegetables and herbs gives them a fine sense of attunement with the nature they love and also imparts the vital sense of self-sufficiency so characteristic of the Norwegian temperament.

## *SAY CHEESE!*

If you're a cheese lover, Norway has much to offer. Norwegian cheeses include Gouda, Gudbrandsdal (Ski Queen), Gamalost, Pultost, Jarlsberg, Ridder, as well as goat milk and dessert cheese varieties.

Both Gouda and Jarlsberg are popular in Norway and abroad. Norwegians like to use them on bread and in pizza, lasagna, and soufflé. The most Norwegian of all cheeses is red cheese. Called Gudbrandsdal, red cheese was first made in Fron in Gudbrandsdalen in the 1850s, and is the most popular cheese on the Norwegian breakfast table. It has a clean, sweet, caramelised flavour.

A word about Gamalost, which is rather special. The name means 'old cheese' and if you smell it, you may understand why it is given this name. Gamalost has roots going back to Viking times, hence its adjective. It is rather granular and has a sharp flavour. Norwegian

Gamalost comes from Hardanger. Unless you have lots of butter to go with it, you may find it hard to eat. Taste it, just to say you have tried it. You may acquire a taste for it.

Another kind of cheese is Aged Norvegia, which has a distinctive black wax covering. It is aged eight to ten months before it is put on the market and has a rich, aromatic, slightly sour flavour. Gomme is cheese that has a sweet whey flavour, with the spiciness of cardamom and cinnamon. It is also an acquired taste.

Norway is also rather well-known for its goat cheeses, which are nut-brown, slightly salty, and faintly goat-flavoured. Goat cheese tastes good on wholemeal bread and *knekkebrød* (Norwegian bran-and-wheat crackers).

There is a very tasty and nutritious processed cheese spread marketed under the brand name Kavli. It is made from hard white cheese that is ground and melted with special salts. Varieties of Kavli are flavoured with bacon, shrimp, ham, and spices.

## THERE'S A FLOWER IN MY SALAD!

Do not droop at the dinner table and ask how that flower got onto your plate. It was most probably very thoughtfully placed in your salad by your Norwegian hostess. Some flowers are edible and taste quite good.

Norwegians also love to grow their own herbs and garnishes in little pots in their kitchen. They will season a chicken with their own rosemary, a lamb dish with marjoram, and a fish dish with dill from their kitchen garden. Nothing gives them greater joy than to use ingredients they have grown themselves. You too may learn to cultivate this habit and develop green fingers. Growing your own herbs is also a good way of ensuring that you have herbs almost the whole year round without having to scout the supermarket or provision store for them.

When we mention salads, we think of lettuce and other greens as a base ingredient. In some parts of Norway, lettuce is not easy to come by and could be quite expensive. Hence, many Norwegians use cabbage in their salads. Norwegian cabbage tastes delicious raw. You won't appreciate this comment until you taste the vegetable yourself. The fact that the vegetables grown in Norway have very few chemicals sprayed on them has something to do with it.

## MUSHROOM PICKING IN THE FORESTS

Norwegians have always been good at taking advantage of what nature has to offer in the way of food. The country's vast spaces are public domain. Farmers might mark their territorial boundaries in the forests but anyone can walk through them.

Some Norwegians enjoy picking mushrooms in the forest. There is an abundance of canterelle mushrooms, golden and delicious when sautéed in butter with garlic. Norwegians are not yet as appreciative of mushrooms as their southern European neighbours, but there is a growing group of enthusiasts among the younger generation.

Going mushroom picking in the forests can double up as a nature walk. If you have lived most of your life in the city, you will be keenly aware of that special light in a clearing of pine trees irradiating the grass with a special greenness; the smell of wood; the rustle of a squirrel scuttling along a branch. Go with a Norwegian friend as a guide. He or she will tell you if a fox has recently been in the same clearing. You sniff the air. At first, you smell nothing unusual. You sniff vigorously again. And there you have it – a faint elusive pungent smell of fox fur.

You should always go with a Norwegian the first time you go into the woods, for then you will learn how to recognise boundary markers and understand how not to get lost. You will probably come unawares suddenly upon a mushroom patch. In excited anticipation, you bend down to gather your yield home, wielding your little sharp knife expertly to cut the mushrooms cleanly at the base.

A word of caution here: you could get very sick if you eat the wrong kinds of mushroom. Get a good guidebook on how to pick the right mushrooms, and go with an expert the first time. You will soon learn to look at the underside of the mushroom – the way the 'weft' goes tells you if the mushroom is edible.

## BERRY PICKING IN THE MOUNTAINS

Autumn is the season of harvests, when Norway's mountains are full of wild berries that are there for the picking. The mountains are resplendent with the purple of blueberries and the striking red of lingonberries. Like the Norwegians, you will find joy in walking in the mountains to pick berries home. Bring buckets to fill and the berry-picking shovels you borrowed from your neighbour. These are designed to sift the berries from the stalks and line them in the shovel for easy collection.

Blueberries are gorgeous when fresh, but also rather delicate. Once you get home with your bucketful, you should immediately borrow another piece of equipment from your neighbour, assuming of course that your neighbour is a regular berry-picker: this is a berry-sorting machine consisting of a hand-operated cylindrical apparatus with slats that allow the berries to go through but retain the larger pieces of twigs and bramble collected along with the berries. You turn the handle of this machine and it revolves slowly, sifting the berries from the leaves and twigs.

Be careful not to stain your clothes with blueberry juice; blueberry stains are impossible to remove. And don't let it bother you if your tongue and lips turn purple-blue for a little while after you have eaten your berries.

Another favourite with berry pickers is the lingonberry or wild cranberries (*tyttebaer*). It is harder and more durable than the blueberry and grows in drier soil. The lingonberry can be collected and dried and then stored to season food – wild game, for example. It can also be made into a good jam.

Most Norwegians buy berries and fruit in season, or even pick them in the countryside, to make jam at home. You can buy the

129

*Out on a berry-picking tour. A Norwegian initiates his Asian friends to the joy of blueberry hunting. Notice the buckets which won't remain empty for long.*

reactive agent for jam-making in the supermarket, with or without preservative. If you cook the jam, it keeps longer, but uncooked berry jam tastes better.

A particular Scandinavian delicacy is the golden cloudberry that grows in swamps and high up in the mountainsides in southern Norway. The supply is not always reliable because the young plants and flowers are very susceptible to frost. The cloudberry thus commands a good price; in rich cloudberry years, a good income is out there, waiting for the picking. Norwegians use cloudberries in jam or eat them fresh with cream on festive occasions such as Christmas Eve.

Wild raspberries are a delight in late summer. They are smaller than the cultivated variety and taste sweeter. Raspberries can be purple-black, red, or yellow. They are easy to pick: just pluck them off their pistils.

## BREAD, FLATBREAD, AND LEFSE

Norwegians are great consumers of bread. Very often, a hungry Norwegian will be happy simply to have several slices of good bread, white or perhaps solid, coarse-grain bread. Norwegians eat bread at least three times a day – at breakfast (*smørbrød*), a packed lunch at school or at work (*nistepakke*), and a slice or two in the evening.

The most important grains in Norway are oats, wheat, rye, and barley. Wheat is the most demanding and is cultivated only in the lowland regions. Rye and oats are not so sensitive while barley, a more robust grain, is grown on mountain farms. Norwegian flour is coarser and contains more of the whole grain than flour in most other countries; coarse flour is what you get from small mills or the tradition of hand-milling.

Bread, usually in the form of flatbread, is frequently served as an accompaniment to meat and fish dishes. In the old days, flatbread and *lefse* were the most important breads. Flatbread dough is made with freshly ground oats and water, kneaded in a large trough, divided into small balls of equal size, and rolled out with grooved or latticed rolling pins into thin round sheets about 50 cm in diameter. They are then rolled onto a thin wooden pin and then rolled out again onto a hot baking stone or griddle to bake. The result is a thin and crispy bread.

*Lefse* is baked hard or soft. Oat *lefse* is made of coarse flour, rolled thick and baked at such low heat that it becomes crisp or hard. Soft *lefse* has a much shorter shelf life as it is made of fine flour and cream, among other things. *Lefse* can be festive food if topped with the right ingredients. The most popular topping is lightly-salted butter and cinnamon sugar. On the west coast, the *lefse* is thin and crisp or soft and thicker. But the filling is what gives this rather bland bread its special taste.

## SALMON, HERRING, AND ALL THAT FISH

In Norway, you will learn about salmon fishing and eating trout and pickled herring. Norway has a long coastline, and the Norwegian coast is marked by mountains, fjords, and a very narrow strip of arable land. The farms along the coast have generally been too small and unproductive to feed a family, and most people have relied on fishing as their primary source of income.

Norwegians have been eating fish for years: mainly cod, herring, trout, brisling, salmon, and mackerel. Norway's economy has grown on its fishing industry. Between 80% and 90% of Norwegian fish is exported. Some cities, including Bergen and Alesund, are closely associated with selling and processing fish and fish products. Bergen has a famous fish market at the quayside where you can buy all sorts of fresh fish; if you are hungry you can also buy smoked salmon sandwiches. In autumn, brisling boats can be seen in the fjords along the west coast, their lights twinkling in the encroaching darkness.

Norwegian fish is sold in many forms: whole or in fillets, frozen or fresh, lightly-salted, salted, smoked, half-dried, salted and dried, marinated and pickled. Until the 1980s, salmon and trout were the most popular fish served on special occasions, but they were seasonal, enjoyed from May to August. Then fish farms changed the dependence on seasons. Today, Norwegian farmed salmon is enjoyed in countries like Japan and the United States of America.

One thing must be said though. Smoked salmon made from wild salmon does taste better than smoked salmon made from farmed salmon. The former has a certain exuberance in flavour lacking in the latter. If you are lucky and come across the fish van from Alesund on its fortnightly round to your town, buy this smoked wild salmon.

Herring is often called the silver of the sea. Harvesting herring can be an uncertain trade as the fish might visit certain coastal areas, only to disappear completely and show up somewhere else. From the 19th century and up to World War II, salt herring or *spekesild* was the most common dinner dish for people of limited means. Nowadays, on the west coast, *spekesild* is sometimes eaten on Saturdays with cranberry sauce, fresh onion slivers, pickled beetroot, and boiled potato. When you first try *spekesild*, you will be overwhelmed by its salty flavour

*At the fish market in Bergen, you can get everything from cooked shrimps to crab in shell and smoked herring.*

and rawness, but once you get used to it, you could find yourself longing for its light taste. Fresh herring, rolled in beaten egg and breadcrumbs, and fried in oil, is quite tasty. The only problem with eating herring is that you have to tackle all those bones as well.

Herring is also canned in a variety of sauces such as lobster, wine, dill, and tomato sauce. These are often sold abroad as *gaffelbiter* or 'tidbits'. You can pickle and marinate salted herring at home using herbs and spices. The supermarket sells small buckets of salt herring (whole or filleted) or herring in brine. Be careful. Do not pickle these herring without soaking in water to remove the salt.

Yet another variety of herring, the *matjes* herring, is probably the best known abroad. It is sometimes sold by weight but more often in cans. These need no previous soaking and may be substituted for salt herring in herring recipes if desired. Whatever variety of herring is used, the marinade should always be cold when it is poured over them.

There is a popular shrimp fished from the Oslo fjord in the south to the big fishing fields in the Barents Sea in the north. These shrimps, sometimes marketed as Greenland Prawns, are rather special in taste and texture. They are caught, cooked, and frozen at sea, and when the shrimp boats arrive, people gather round to buy newly cooked, succulent shrimps. Some of the shrimps have roe and it is an experience to suck the roe and eat the sweetish-tender meat with fresh white bread, mayonnaise, and lemon. If you are in luck, you may be invited to a shrimp party where the main course is shrimps eaten in the way just described, washed down with *pils*.

## NORWEGIAN DELICACIES

### Lutefisk

For a few weeks before Christmas, restaurants serve a hearty meal of *lutefisk* with stewed green or yellow peas, or white sauce with mustard, or even melted pork fat and fried bacon. Norwegians eat this lean fish with *lefse* or flatbread. *Lutefisk* is an acquired taste. You either love it or hate it at first sight!

*Lutefisk* is cod soaked in lye-water (a soda solution) for two to three days to soften. The fish is ready when a finger can be pressed through a medium-thick fillet without resistance. The cod is then soaked in running cold water for two days, until all the lye is rinsed out. It is cut into rather large serving pieces, which are boiled or poached. Most Norwegians enjoy at least one *lutefisk* dinner before Christmas. *Lutefisk* season is the coldest and darkest time of the year.

### Finnish Beef

This is probably the best known Sami specialty for the average Norwegian. Chances are that you will get to try it at least once during your stay in Norway. Thinly shave reindeer meat (either bought already shaved or shaved with a sharp knife from a half-frozen reindeer shoulder) is browned in butter and seasoned with salt and

Lutefisk *with boiled potatoes, a Norwegian delicacy you will either love or hate.*

pepper. When the meat begins to colour, chopped onion is added and cooked until golden. The dish is rounded off with sour cream, a few slices of brown goat cheese and crushed juniper berries. After a few minutes' simmering, it is ready to serve with boiled or mashed potatoes and lingonberry compote.

## Salted Lamb Ribs – Pinnekjøtt

*Pinnekjøtt* means twig meat. The rather unusual name refers to the rack of birch twigs in the bottom of the pan that is used to steam the ribs. The meat needs to be steamed for two to three hours to be tender and juicy. *Pinnekjøtt* is a Christmas delicacy and it is always a treat to have it served piping hot on warm plates, in its own juice, with mashed rutabaga and boiled potatoes. *Pinnekjøtt* can be expensive, and if you want to have it for a party, you must have enough to go around, and have the time to cook it well.

## THE NORWEGIAN BUFFET TABLE – SMØRGÅSBORD

Most foreign visitors to Norway go home with a lasting impression of the fascinating buffet tables that typify Norwegian hospitality. In summer, most hotels serve buffets daily, and on special occasions, buffet tables are set up at home to entertain guests. The Norwegian buffet table or *smørgåsbord* is a fascinating array of cold and hot dishes that delight the eye and please the palate. When you are in Norway, you must sample a *smørgåsbord* meal to know why tourists talk about it.

You will probably encounter your first Norwegian buffet at the hotel breakfast table. Norwegians believe in a hearty breakfast, and a roll and jam just won't do for a hungry Norwegian. A Norwegian breakfast buffet will have different kinds of bread, milk and juice, cereal, cold cuts, eggs, cheese, jam, marmalade, and little jars of pickled herring in sherry or mustard marinade. The Norwegian buffet lunch boasts a similar array, added to which are fish and shellfish dishes, dried meats with side dishes, hot dishes made with fish, meat, and occasionally pasta, salads with dressings, and desserts like ice cream, caramel and chocolate puddings, Bavarian creams, cakes, berries, and fruit.

Actually, *smørgåsbord* is a Swedish word for the famous Scandinavian buffet table laden with a multitude of different dishes, mainly cold, ranging from spicy cured herrings and other fish, through meats and salads, to cheeses. The word literally means 'bread-and-butter table', the idea being that you help yourself from the various dishes and eat the bread and butter with these. The Danish and Norwegian name is *koldt bord*, which means 'cold table', but *smørgåsbord* is the better-known name and has remained to distinguish this type of buffet.

The idea of the *smørgåsbord* is said to have originated in Sweden at country parties long ago, when the guests would bring their own dishes and set these out on their hostess's table, together with her contributions – a kind of potluck gathering. Later on, this idea of collective contributions died out, leaving the hostess to prepare her own buffet table herself.

Whatever the scale of the *smørgåsbord*, there is a certain ritual attached to eating from it. It is the custom to begin with the various cured herring before you change your plate for the salads and the meats, and if you have room for it, a small warm dish before finishing up with the cheese. You should definitely not put all the herrings, delicate patés, mayonnaise salads, and cheeses on the same plate. Various kinds of bread such as Danish rye bread, white bread, Norwegian wafer-thin *flatbrød*, and *knekkebrød* or crispbread accompany the hot and cold dishes on a Norwegian buffet table.

The drink that goes down well with *smørgåsbord* is schnapps, *aquavit*, or beer. Schnapps is sometimes served in the traditional *kluflaske* (distinctive glasses with exceptionally long and hollow stems), so called because of the gurgling sound it makes when you pour from it.

## THE NORWEGIAN MAIN COURSE

The main meal of the day for Norwegians is *middag* – the only hot meal in the day. *Middag* is dinner, which is normally eaten at 5 p.m. In the countryside, *middag* takes place a little earlier, at 4 p.m.

At *middag*, it is important that the entire family sits down to the meal together. This is one main focus for family interaction. Parents and children may have their routines, but at dinnertime, they all sit down together to give thanks for the food and to see each other. Most Norwegians serve only one main course for dinner. Learn what it is that Norwegians eat because soon you, too, may be serving it to your own family.

### Meatballs in Brown Sauce

*Kjøttkaker* or Norwegian meatballs are a common staple in the Norwegian diet. Norwegian children love it. It is made of minced beef seasoned with salt, pepper, a touch of ginger, potato flour, and milk, then formed into patties and fried until golden-brown. You only need to brown the meatballs, not cook them thoroughly. (If you happen to make *kjøttkaker*, do them in a bigger bulk so you can deepfreeze some for later use.) Next, make a brown sauce from the oil left behind, adding flour, milk, and soup stock, or use an instant brown sauce mix. Simmer the meatballs in the brown gravy and serve them with boiled potatoes.

Norwegians have been known to be so fond of their meatballs that some of them holidaying abroad brought along cans of meatballs in brown sauce – just in case the food on their travels did not agree with their stomachs!

## Lamb Stew with Cabbage

*Fårikål* is a traditional Norwegian dish in the autumn when mutton is abundant (it is slaughter time for sheep then). It would be wise to buy your mutton then and store it in your freezer – the mutton is fresh and its price is low.

This stew is a heavy dish, very solid and nourishing. The chunks of mutton are put in a pot and boiled with wedges of cabbage, peppercorns, salt, and a bayleaf or two, for a couple of hours. The cabbage becomes soggy, but that is the way it should be. The meat is tender and the stew is rich and soupy. Delicious – with boiled potatoes, of course.

## Fishballs in White Sauce

If you have never tried Norwegian fishballs or *fiskeboller*, your first time is a truly gastronomic experience. For the Asian foreigner used to fishballs made wholly from fishmeat and boiled in soup, Norwegian fishballs are a rude shock. The Asian fishball is springy in texture and contains only fish, salt, and water. The Norwegian fishball is soft and milky, both in colour and flavour. It is an acquired taste, but you could get fond of it.

You can buy fish pudding in the supermarket and cut it into slices to fry and eat just like that. Or buy the ready-made *fiskefarse* or fishball mixture and form your own fishballs to drop into boiling water to cook. Make a white sauce of butter or margarine, flour, and milk, and add a bouillon cube – and you have *fiskeboller* in white sauce!

## Lapskaus *or Potato and Meat Stew*

*Lapskaus*, a favourite with children and adults, is a traditional and well-balanced dish. It may be light or dark, depending on the way it is prepared. Light *lapskaus* is sometimes called salt *lapskaus*, indicating that salted meat (it should be soaked before cooking) and perhaps a little salt pork is used. But *lapskaus* should never be salty.

To make *lapskaus*, throw cubed potatoes, carrots, sliced leek, sausage, and any meat leftovers all together into water to make a soupy stew that is warm and good, especially in winter. 'Brown' *lapskaus* is made with primarily leftover cooked meat, boiled potatoes, and a little gravy. *Lapskaus* can also be made in bulk and frozen in portions to eat on other days.

## USING A FREEZER

You will find that the freezer is a necessity for the family. You can stock up on summer vegetables for the winter, when cabbage, potato, and carrot are the main staple vegetables. What a delight it is to be able to have squash in winter, or a broccoli with cheese sauce, or brussels sprouts with your beefsteak.

In autumn, when you and your neighbours share an entire deer sold by a nearby farmer, freeze chunks of venison for later use – in the freezer. When your neighbour goes fishing and returns with a pail of trout for you, clean the fish, cook some the same day, and save the rest for later – in the freezer. When you cook a hotpot, and have a lovely assortment of meat, potatoes, and leek that the family cannot finish, store the remainder in a container in the freezer and take it out another day when you run out of cooking ideas, or don't feel like cooking, or simply fancy having mutton stew again.

Most Norwegian women work today and the freezer is a great aid. In the autumn fruit season, berry-pickers return from the forest laden with bucketfuls of blueberries or lingonberries. They make blueberry pies and store the rest of the berries in the freezer. When your neighbour invites you over to pick berries from his *solbaer* (sunberry) bushes or you go to the farms and pluck strawberries and cherries to take home for a fee, you know you can take home a whole bulk of your favourite fruit and be able to eat them again and again, not necessarily at one go, because you have the freezer.

## STOCKING YOUR KITCHEN

You probably moved to Norway with all your pots and pans from your last kitchen in another part of the world. On the other hand, settling in Norway may mean starting from scratch. Here is a list of things that might help if you wish to learn the Norwegian lifestyle:

- A cast-iron, enamel-lined casserole with a tightly fitting lid that can be reversed for use as a heavy frying pan or saucepan. Meat and fowl are often roasted on top of the cooker in such a casserole, the oven not being used all that often for this purpose. The meat cooks in its own juices and is tender and succulent. The casserole is also practical for serving direct from the cooker to the table.
- Oblong bread tins – useful if you want to learn to bake bread – also do double duty as cake tins.
- Wooden or glass bowls for salads, boards for cheese and meat, and small individual wooden boards beside each plate for buttering bread, biscuits, or crispbread. The last items are an interesting and more manageable alternative to using the usual plate with a raised edge for buttering bread.
- A food processor or a mincer for meat or vegetables. When you buy your meat in bulk, it is handy to have a food processor to cut up your meat into mince for storage in the freezer.

- A birch whisk for smooth sauces is really a most useful tool to ensure no unsightly lumps in soups or sauces that use flour as a thickener.
- A sharp, half-moon-shaped chopper – known by its Italian name, Mezzaluna – is useful for chopping almonds, parsley, and other choppable edibles.
- A waffle iron for making Scandinavian waffles, delicious with sour cream and freshly-made fruit jam.
- A ring-shaped mould – an attractive shape for serving a number of savoury and sweet dishes, such as aspic or a light chocolate cake.
- A cheese slicer. Many Scandinavian cheeses have a firm, smooth texture, and are best cut in thin slices for open sandwiches.

## *YOU'RE INVITED TO DINNER!*

You have held your first social event of the year. You have invited your Norwegian neighbours over for dinner.

But now that you have had your first dinner party, you wonder when you will be invited over. You wait and wait. While you are waiting, it seems to you that Norwegians procrastinate in inviting guests over to their house.

Norwegians are not unsociable, they are simply very house-proud. What happens is that they feel their homes must be clean and beautiful before they can invite people over. And when they cook their meal, they choose a good meat, set out the finest crockery, and lay out the crystal glasses for the wine. Naturally, it takes some time before they invite you over since both your neighbours are working full-time. Moreover, when summer comes, most Norwegians are busy enjoying the sun and the season and therefore seldom issue formal invitations to dinner. If any invitations come in summer, they are usually for light, casual, informal affairs – a barbecue or a simple pie-and-salad meal out on the balcony perhaps.

The invitation for dinner finally arrives. What should you bring for your hosts?

Bring a little plant. Norwegian women love to have something green and growing in their homes, and plants are always appreciated. Especially when someone is settling into a new home and you are invited to a housewarming, a plant in a pot makes a good gift. In fact, when you first invited your Norwegian friends over for a meal, they might have brought you a little plant as a gift.

Flowers are also a good present. You could visit the local florist or nursery to buy a bouquet. If children are invited, they can bring along their little bouquets gathered that afternoon from the garden or along the roadside. Norwegians appreciate little thoughtful gestures, and when children give them a gift from the heart, they will reciprocate with warmth and joy. Even wildflowers plucked from the roadside will be accepted with sincerity and your hostess will find a little vase or bottle to put them in. (Incidentally, always check with your hosts, if you are uncertain, whether your children have been invited to dinner. Unless it is stated that your family is invited, only you and your spouse should accept the invitation.)

Chocolates are a traditionally safe gift to bring. They probably will have chocolates with the coffee after dinner, and your gift may be added to the chocolate tray. If you happen to have some souvenirs or gifts from your home country, all the better. A batik tablecloth would be much admired and a Chinese cloisonne trinket would be proudly displayed on the mantelpiece. Norwegians are quite interested in other cultures and appreciate exotica. They might not like the taste of some exotic foods (it all depends on which part of Norway they come from – some regions are more conservative than others), but your gesture will be appreciated.

Make sure you arrive on time for dinner. When Norwegians specify that dinner is at 7 p.m., it is at 7 p.m. They would have prepared a roast to be just ready for the tasting at that time; overheating would result in a tired roast. So observe punctuality.

You will be greeted with pecks on the cheek and great warmth, and ushered to the dinner table almost immediately. Norwegians do not

*Norwegians take time and trouble to prepare their table for guests. This one bears typical festive fare:* kransekake *(almond ring-cake), which requires a considerable time to bake.*

usually stand around drinking cocktails unless they are at an official function. At home, dinner is served immediately the guest arrives, and conversation sails around the dinner table and continues over coffee and cake. Sometimes, a liqueur is served with the coffee.

*Skål!* This is the Norwegian equivalent of 'Cheers!' or 'Bottoms up!' Norwegians usually serve a wine with their dinner and your host will inevitably, at the commencement of dinner, raise his wineglass and make a toast. *Skål!* You raise your glass too and share in the toasting. *Skål* is always heard when Norwegians are drinking together or anticipating a pleasant evening together in good company.

When you are invited to dinner, be prepared to stay at least a couple of hours. Norwegians take time to socialise. Dinner may start at 7 p.m. and end at 10:30 p.m. It all depends on the company and how scintillating the social interaction becomes. You will find Norwegians very relaxed at home, playing host. And you will go away from the meal feeling a certain satisfaction and a sense of well-being. It was a good dinner.

## INGRID ESPELID

When talking about Norwegian cuisine, it is impossible not to mention the name Ingrid Espelid-Høvig in the same breath. Ingrid Espelid is so famous that every Norwegian who knows his potatoes and meatballs will know of her. She is acknowledged as *hele Norges matmor* – literally, the food mother of the whole of Norway.

Ingrid Espelid is the one who tells Norwegians how long they should roast their meats and how much spice to use in one dish. Having spent about three decades on NRK TV, this small, almost diminutive woman with the twinkling eye and gentle smile is no stranger to exotic spices and new tastes. In 1956, she started a food programme on television. Today, her *Fjernsynskjøkkenet* (*TV Kitchen*) programme makes the rounds of countries as far-flung as Hungary to Thailand, America to Africa.

Ingrid has talked about, tasted, and explored the world's dishes on Norwegian television, and she is recognised today as almost a Norwegian institution. Who knows? You might even find yourself following her programme and trying out her recipes in your own kitchen, if you happen to be in Norway.

Ingrid Espelid has also published numerous cookbooks which are admired for their clarity and simplicity.

## TAKE YOUR PICK

Norwegian food culture has changed over the years. Eating habits have followed the times, and pizza and spaghetti can now be found on the plates of most Norwegians. Fast foods, however, have never really caught on in Norway – it took McDonald's some years before it hit the

Oslo scene. Chinese restaurants, on the other hand, are gaining popularity.

Norway has very stringent standards for food outlets and are very aware of consumer protection. All foods sold in the supermarket carry their expiry date. The law requires that the contents or composition of the product be clearly stated on the package. Tinned food, including imported products, are closely monitored for these reasons.

Norwegians are a people who eat to live. Food for them has been, to a large extent, functional. There is some form and ritual when it comes to preparing food and having a party, but on the whole, Norwegians are simple in their culinary tastes. They appreciate good food but will not go out to search for new restaurants serving the latest and most exotic dishes. When friends are invited, the atmosphere is more important than the food.

# Chapter Five

# BRINGING CHILDREN TO NORWAY

Bringing children to Norway adds another dimension to adjustment and adaptation. Children have special requirements, a primary one of which is education. This chapter will explore some of the main issues relating to children in Norway.

## *FINDING A SCHOOL*

The first thing to do is to check out the education system and the schooling opportunities for your children. You can do this in several ways. Some of your office colleagues or neighbours may have children of school-going age and be able to offer useful advice. You could also visit the local education authority. Yet another way is to locate a teacher in the neighbourhood or visit the nearest school. If it is within walking distance, walk there one school day and see the principal. Explain your situation and you will be told how you can register your children.

Schooling is compulsory in Norway. National provisions regarding compulsory education have existed in Norway since the mid-18th century. In 1889, the Storting adopted legislation regarding compulsory seven-year schooling for everyone. From World War II, high priority was given to ensure that all children received an equal education, regardless of where they lived in Norway. Then, in 1969, a landmark primary and secondary school legislation removed disparities between urban and rural school programmes, and increased compulsory education to nine years. All children aged 7 to 16 who live in Norway for more than three months have the right and the duty to attend school.

Once your children are registered and have begun school, you should observe some basic rules. If they are sick and cannot attend school, inform the school authorities. If your children are travelling out of the country during the school term, inform the authorities and seek permission for their absence. If your family is planning to relocate to another place in Norway or abroad, you must also show the courtesy of keeping the school and the local education department informed.

## LANGUAGE INSTRUCTION

You are your children's best role model, and your willingness to adapt to the country's milieu will be an example you will want to set. What better way than through learning Norwegian?

Norway has accepted many immigrants and, as part of the adjustment process for them, has provided a minimum number of hours in the instruction of the main medium of communication in Norway, Norwegian. As an adult foreigner, you are entitled to 240 hours of a free introductory Norwegian language instruction course. (Refugees and other adults who have been given a residence permit on humanitarian grounds are offered 500 hours tuition free of charge.) This is a bonus for those keen on adapting in a new country, so enrol in the basic course. Once the teacher gets an adequate minimum number of students, the class will begin. Classes are usually held in a school building.

Your children will receive extra hours of tuition in the Norwegian language by their class teacher or another teacher trained in speech therapy. (If one of them has speech problems, this therapist will be a great help.) In school, your children will be relating to the class in Norwegian. In the beginning, it is like throwing them into the deep end of a pool. But you will be amazed at the amount of learning that goes on subconsciously. The form teacher is also the English teacher and can adequately interpret for your child initially.

## Help in Communication

If there is an initial barrier in communication with a Norwegian, know that you can have access to an interpreter. Foreigners have the same right to give and receive information as Norwegians. It is the responsibility of the authorities to ensure that foreigners receive information in such a way that they can make use of it. If foreigners who cannot read Norwegian cannot be provided with information written in their mother tongue, the authorities see to it that the information is conveyed to them verbally through an interpreter.

An interesting development with regard to language communication is the Nordic Language Convention, which came into force in 1987. It entitles citizens of other Nordic countries to use their own languages when dealing with the Norwegian authorities. The convention applies to the Danish, Swedish, Norwegian, Finnish, and Icelandic languages, and covers both verbal and written contact, but not telephone calls. In accordance with the convention, the cost of interpretation should be covered by the public authorities.

## *Language Teaching in Upper Secondary Schools*

Upper secondary schools offer a core curriculum that includes a compulsory second foreign language as well as English. There is freedom of choice as to which foreign language is studied. In practice, the majority of schools offer German, French, and (to some extent) Spanish. In the upper secondary schools, the terms used for language learning are 'A-, B-, and C-languages':

- The A-language is English. The foundation course in the A-language is based on the normal six years of language study in primary and lower secondary schools.
- The B-language is the foreign language pupils have studied in addition to English in lower secondary school, and which they continue to study in upper secondary school. Foundation courses in B-languages are based on the normal two years of study in lower secondary school.
- The C-language is the foreign language pupils start learning in upper secondary school. It can be the student's second or third foreign language. Foundation courses in C-languages are beginners' courses.

You have to know at which levels your children fit in. Discuss with the school authorities the appropriate levels for your children to enter Norwegian schools.

## *Instruction in a Second Language and the Mother Tongue*

Norwegian children begin learning a second language, usually English, from Primary 4 onwards. Before this, they receive instruction in one medium only, Norwegian. This means that all students, foreign or Norwegian, must go through 3 years of education in the Norwegian medium of instruction. This is not a discriminatory practice enforced to make it difficult for foreigners to follow classes. Rather, the intention is to ensure a firm grounding in Norwegian language, the mother tongue for Norwegians. It is perceived as being very important that Norwegians are able to understand and be understood in their own tongue before they go on to grapple with the intricacies of another language.

Foreigners who enter the local system will find that children adapt remarkably well. Within a few weeks of attending school in Norwegian, do not be surprised if your children begin uttering strange sentences in a foreign tongue that you cannot understand. Children at play learn a language well informally because speech patterns are reinforced as your children imitate other children. The education system includes specially trained counsellors and other special advisors who can guide and help foreign children if they flounder.

As for instruction in the mother tongue for foreign students, a special clause written into the Education Act states that every foreign child has the right to learn his or her own mother tongue. The state will pay the salary of the instructor, but sometimes it works out in such a way, politically, that the municipality has to pay. You will have to check this out with your local education office.

The reality is that it is difficult, if not impossible, to find a teacher of Greek, for example, for a Greek child living in a small town in Norway. Certainly, the child's parents could be an important source when learning the mother tongue.

## NORWEGIAN EDUCATION IN A NUTSHELL

Norwegian children begin school at the age of 7 years, but there is talk of starting them earlier. Basic education lasts 9 years. All schooling is coeducational, and there is no official policy to segregate the sexes. If this or anything else is in conflict with your religion or culture, discuss your problem with the principal or school counsellor. But expect to have to adjust to the system in Norway.

The Norwegian educational system is divided into four main branches: primary and lower secondary school for students aged 7–16; upper secondary school, offering students aged 16–19 an academic, a vocational, or combined academic-vocational education;

*Norwegian children accept and welcome children of other races and nationalities. Peer group influence is a very strong pressure group in Norway, especially among teenagers.*

colleges (commonly referred to as *høgskoler*) and universities for higher education; and an extensive adult education programme providing courses at all educational levels. Primary and lower secondary schools are administered at municipal level, while upper secondary schools are the responsibility of the county authorities. Colleges and universities have a centralised administration at state level.

The majority of students in Norway are educated at public institutions. Although private schools exist to some degree at all educational levels, these institutions also receive public funding. You will not have to pay for your children's place in school. Schooling is free in Norway, up to the tertiary level. This means that there is no such thing as school fees. Students have to buy only their school books, and they can usually get them secondhand from past students or even borrow them from friends and neighbours. Since education is free and compulsory, attendance is closely monitored to make sure all students attend class regularly.

## *Grades and Levels*

In primary school, there are no marks or examinations. It is believed that children learn best without pressure.

After 3 years of lower secondary school, an examination is held. Both the examination marks and the marks for overall achievement recorded on the leaving certificate decide whether students can gain a place of choice in upper secondary school. However, foreign students and Norwegian students with special difficulties can be admitted on special grounds. There are also English upper secondary schools in big cities like Oslo and Stavanger; you should check them out to see if your child could be enrolled and how much it will cost.

Higher education includes all training after upper secondary school. The oldest academic institution in Norway is the University of Oslo, founded in 1811. New universities were opened after World War II, in Bergen, Trondheim, and Tromsø. There are several other institutions offering higher education degrees including the Norwegian College of Agriculture at Ås near Oslo, the Norwegian College of Economics and Business Administration in Bergen, the Norwegian State Academy of Music, the Norwegian College of Veterinary Medicine, the Norwegian College of Sport and Physical Education, and the Oslo School of Architecture.

Universities and colleges in Norway have dual functions as teaching and research institutions. The four universities grant degrees at three levels: lower degree (4-year course), higher degree (5- to 7-year course), and a doctorate. You may decide to pursue a higher degree in Norway while staying there, so explore the possibilities for a degree in the subject or area you want. Most university and college professors are quite accessible for advice, if you write to them.

# *STUDENT COUNSELLING*

If you have a child with problems at school, do not be overwhelmed by the immensity of your problem. Norway has a competent student counselling programme in every school. Each school is visited by trained therapists, psychologists, or counsellors who can advise both you and your child. There is no social stigma attached to consultancy with these professionals.

Don't despair if your child has adjustment or reading problems. Norwegian children, many of whom may come from broken homes or have relocated from different parts of Norway, have the same problems. (Norway has a high divorce rate, and some people have tried to circumvent this by cohabiting instead of getting married.)

## FACILITIES FOR HANDICAPPED CHILDREN

A handicapped child can make use of Norway's special privileges for such children. It has been a continuing policy in Norway to integrate children of all capabilities into the regular education system. Norwegian society emphasises equal opportunity, sometimes to the detriment of exceptional children with special needs. What equality means is that children retarded either physically or mentally are encouraged to join the normal classes, usually with their therapist present.

This attempt at integration is noteworthy and the class in general benefits from interaction with handicapped students. Classmates learn patience and appreciation of their own lot. When they see a paraplegic or an autistic child, they learn that many things – like running or talking in smooth, connected sentences – should not be taken for granted.

Integration is good for the process of socialisation, but in practice, it sometimes slows down the teaching process. As the teacher is a considerate educator who wants to make sure everyone learns and absorbs lessons, his or her patience with the handicapped student could lead to impatience and boredom on the part of children who find the pace too slow. A happy balance needs to be found.

## ABOVE-AVERAGE STUDENTS

As Norway believes in the egalitarian principle, no special privileges are granted to exceptional students. While slow learners are given additional assistance to make the grade, students who are above average are not encouraged to surpass the normal grade and develop at their own accelerated pace.

## The Jante Law

In the 1960s, Norwegian poet Aksel Sandemose gave voice to an expression of the Norwegian psyche. His statement has lived on as the Jante law. Basically, the law is based on envy and, at the same time, an anti-elitist principle. It goes like this: 'Don't you believe that you are better than anybody else.'

It is obvious that the Jante law served to retard the unequal growth and development potential of young Norwegians who showed the capacity to excel, whether academically, in sports, or in business. Bright sparks, those exceptionally physically and intellectually gifted, were not allowed to shine for long because schools generally did not recognise their needs or cater to them. The Jante law has helped stifle the growth of burgeoning talent in a way that the egalitarian principle never intended.

But the situation is changing. The present education system evolved from a content-based learning approach in the 1960s, through a liberal phase in the 1970s when the classroom was perceived as one big play area with competition totally eliminated because it was deemed unhealthy, to the mid-1980s when Norway suddenly realised it needed a balance in its orientation towards educating its young. Today, Norway strives to keep a happy equilibrium between nurturing the less intellectually and physically endowed and developing the full potential of the above-average Norwegian.

## THE CHILDREN'S OMBUDSMAN

Norway is very aware of, and concerned about, the welfare of the child. A protracted parliamentary discussion throughout the 1970s on how Norway could best take care of the interests of children in a democracy resulted in the creation of the world's first children's ombudsman, otherwise known as the Commissioner for Children, on 1 September 1981.

According to the Commissioner for Children Act, the ombudsman's duties are 'to promote the interests of children regarding public and private authorities and to follow up the development of conditions under which children grow up'. The ombudsman may act on his own initiative or at the inquiry of other people. He decides whether an application offers sufficient grounds for action.

Administratively, the ombudsman is under the Ministry for Children and Family Affairs. The children's ombudsman has no sanctional power, but at the same time he is seldom neglected by the authorities. He is safeguarded by his own legislation and the long tradition and fine reputation that ombudsmen generally have in Norway. The high moral and professional quality of the ombudsman's work entails his involvement in political issues, but not party politics.

How can you or your children use the children's ombudsman in Norway?

You would probably not use the ombudsman at all, but it is good to know his function and be aware of what he means to Norwegian children. The ombudsman has a high public profile as the children's spokesman on issues important to them. A special television slot gave the ombudsman a weekly 8-minute exposure. After more than a hundred television programmes, he switched to being part of a popular weekly radio programme in 1993. On television and radio, the ombudsman reads out the latest cases his office has handled and the letters he receives from children about issues ranging from a dangerous play area in their neighbourhood and lack of special education services and supervision in foster homes to unsatisfactory visitation conditions for children with a parent in jail and conditions for children in families with alcoholics.

A special communication system was also established. *Klar Melding* (Clear Message) is a hotline telephone system where anyone under 18 years of age can call the ombudsman's telephone answering service, free of charge, and ask any question or present any kind of problem. Many of these have been taken up and answered in the ombudsman's television and radio shows. The children's hotline is mainly used by those aged 10–14, but it is hoped that older children will use it more.

The present children's ombudsman in Norway sees his role embracing three main priorities: child welfare, children and school, and children and health. His work is twofold: he gathers information from individuals applying to the ombudsman, from the research communities, and from professional literature; and he approaches the different levels of the power structure and confronts them with problems, criticism, and proposals for change.

His office is engaged in a diverse range of issues including children and municipal planning, the rights of refugee children, childcare institutions, and family judicial issues – particularly visitation and divorce issues and sexual violence towards children.

Adults who contact the commissioner are mostly concerned with two problems – dissatisfaction with a ruling by the child welfare authorities, placing a children under public care, and problems concerning children after a divorce.

If your children are unclear about certain practices they see their friends, foreign or Norwegian, experiencing, they can use the children's hotline to make an enquiry. Or if you, as a parent, are witness to knowledge about someone else abusing a child, you can ring the ombudsman to lodge a statement of concern. He will make the necessary investigation with the relevant authorities.

## ORGANISING A CHILDREN'S PARTY

Ordinarily, you would go to the bookstore to look for the usual party invitation cards. But then you learn from Norwegian friends that children prefer to make their own cards: it is more personal, fun, and involves the child's imagination and initiative. And so you ask your child to make his or her own cards. Your child might like the colour black, in which case all the invitation cards may be based on a black background. Never mind. Norwegians appreciate originality. All your child has to do is state the time, place, and date and sign off. There is no need to include an RSVP footnote although it would be wise to leave your home contact number for parents to reach you.

In Norway, children come to a party in their finery and expect a good time. This means drinking *brus* (fizzy sodas), eating hot dogs, spaghetti with sausage in tomato or meat sauce, homemade pizza, open sandwiches, raisin buns, waffles with cream and jam, potato chips and other snacks, and rounding off with a chocolate or cream cake, wonderfully decorated with Smarties or interesting little fancifuls, and maybe even ice-cream or jelly. To top it all, it means going home with a bagful of candies (*godteri*). This is the life!

Organising a children's party is relatively easy. You do not have to hunt for the nearest McDonald's to host the party. You have it at home. Remember that Norwegian kids come on time to a party and leave on time too, usually. They love to play games. Try universal games like passing the parcel or treasure hunt, but you can also share some games unique to your own culture.

The main preparation involved is cleaning the house and getting the food ready. Norwegian children will come to your house in their walking shoes, which could be galoshes on a rainy autumn day or snow-caked boots in the deep of winter. They enter your house, leave their walking shoes in the gangway, and put on their neat and quite immaculate party shoes – no padding around in bare feet, so there is no need to mop your house perfectly clean before the party starts.

Make sure there is lots of space. If the children are playing indoors, invite the guests to go to your child's room to play or look at the gifts he or she has received. This gives you time to clean up the food tables before they descend for the next round of eating. Birthday cakes are usually baked by the birthday child's mother. If you or your cake really can't rise to the occasion, go out to the local confectionary and buy one. It helps to place an order in advance.

*Children in Norway always dress for the weather – and are always ready for ice-cream, even in the cold!*

The birthday child plays host. He or she is encouraged to look after the guests and engage them in interesting activities. This of course depends on the age of the birthday child.

Parents usually deposit their children at your doorstep and pick them up again at the stipulated time. If you would like to interact with the parents, invite them to come half-an-hour earlier to pick up their children. The party should be running on its own steam by then, and you will have time to sit and drink coffee with the adults. If it is a toddler's party, mothers are usually present to look after their little ones. Sharing of responsibilities and exchange of opinions about child-rearing, the education system, the local kindergarten scene, and so on naturally follows.

Most parents who come earlier to have coffee with you do not expect a lot of food. They would have had their dinner since most children's parties take place after dinner, which is 4–5 p.m. Hot coffee or tea and some cake are more than adequate sustenance for visiting parents at the party.

## USING A BICYCLE HELMET

Bicycling is a favourite pastime in Norway. Most Norwegian children who live in the suburbs or countryside are used to riding a bicycle to school. When you live in Norway, invest in a bicycle for your child. It makes visiting friends, going to school, and having exercise all that much simpler. In Norway, there are specially designated lanes on the roads for cyclists.

Children are taught traffic safety at an early age. Sometimes the local traffic police representative gives talks on the subject in schools. One of the rules covered at length is the use of bicycle helmets.

All cyclists must use bicycle helmets for protection against injury when cycling. Head injuries have been identified as the most common and serious result of bad falls from bicycles. One-third of all cycling injuries treated by doctors are head injuries. Consumer protection laws ensure that your child's helmet is a legitimate form of protection.

When you choose a helmet, pay close attention to its features. A good bicycle helmet sits well on the head. Many types come only in two or three sizes, but with a suitable cushion or padding, you can adjust the size. If your child happens to have a big head and the helmet is too small, you could remove some of the extra padding. The helmet should not hinder sight or hearing, and it should be possible to use spectacles with the helmet on the head. A hard helmet – one with a harder outer layer than the usual polystyrene – seems to offer better protection. The helmet should tolerate regular cleaning. (Don't, however, paint it or apply chemicals when cleaning it, since its material may react chemically paint of special cleaning agents.)

Helmets that satisfy the basic safety requirements bear a stamp of approval from the authorities. Bicycle helmets can also double up as skateboard helmets.

## CHILDREN IN THE CAR

In 1 October 1988, a law came into effect stipulating that all children under the age of 15 years should have seatbelts when driven in a car.

Norwegians are rather careful drivers and child safety is a prime consideration. There is a section of the traffic police department, known as *Trygg Trafikk*, concerned with traffic safety. It issues the latest rules and information pertaining to safer road usage and is a most helpful source for queries on any aspect of road safety.

If you are driving with a baby in the car, you should attach the baby seat to the front seat, facing towards the backseat. Research has proven that this is the safest position for infants in a car. Children below 11 years old are encouraged to use the seatbelt, preferably on a raised safety cushion, for comfort.

It would seem that if you have a family of six, you might have problems transporting the entire family in the same car since Norwegian law states that only five people may travel safely in one car. Of course, if you own a station-wagon or a mini-van, your problem is solved. Indeed, look into the possibility of getting a mini-bus. Couples with four or six children can happily trundle the family around Norwegian and other European roads in a mini-bus or van. If you decide to buy a mini-bus, make sure you get a special driving licence for vehicles in that category. Getting one is easy if you enrol in a driving school and get the required hours of instruction.

## *CHILDREN'S ROOMS*

Children in Norwegian homes, particularly teenage children, usually get a bedroom of their own. If you have more than one child, consider setting off one part of the house or apartment near their bedrooms as a children's corner. This ensures that you get some privacy when your children's friends come to visit, as they will, usually after dinner. The same area could be used to store the children's toys, on shelves or in little boxes, and a library of children's books. Children need their own space, and recognising this need is important to their development of self-esteem and responsibility. They must have space to entertain their friends, just as you entertain yours.

## FINDING CHILDCARE FACILITIES

When you arrive in Norway with a preschool child, one of your primary concerns will be to identify the nearest playgroup, creche, playschool, or kindergarten. If you intend to look after your child yourself, all the better. Child-rearing in Norway is perceived as a joint responsibility and couples are granted maternity and paternity leave, whatever the case may be, to look after their children.

One of the best ways to find a playgroup is to ask the neighbours. If you are lucky, you might find you are residing in a neighbourhood that has children of about the same age as your child. Having a social group of mothers is most comforting, particularly when you are settling in. A feeling of alienation generally affects women who stay at home alone with their children.

There is a choice of childcare facilities, depending on your need.

### Playgroup

It is not uncommon to find a group of housewives in a neighbourhood forming a regular playgroup with their toddlers. They meet in each other's homes once a week and could even have lunch gatherings. Tell someone you know that you are interested in joining or even starting an informal playgroup and you will be surprised how quickly the word goes round. Before you know it, you have a group of new friends.

### Dagmamma

If you are a working mother who needs someone to look after your child when you are not at home, a *dagmamma* (literally, day mother) is what you should look for. A *dagmamma* is a foster mother of sorts.

She could be your next-door neighbour who volunteers to take on the responsibility of looking after your child in the daytime. Even if she and you are friends, as a rule you pay her a regular fee worked out by the hour. When you have your neighbour as a *dagmamma*, you have the advantage of knowing your child is secure, happy, and in safe hands.

161

A *dagmamma* may be found by word of mouth. She could live some distance away. It is advisable to interview someone new and to visit her home because this is where your child will be for the better part of some days. You should be aware if she is a smoker because you do not want to expose your child to the dangers of passive smoking. Bring your child with you for this first visit to see how they relate together. Matching your child with a care-giver is very important.

## Barnepark

You can park your child in a 'children's park' or *barnepark*. A *barnepark* is based on the concept of outdoor activities for children in a daycare playground. Usually, children are left there to play for half the day, under the supervision of adults.

Equip your *barnepark* child with the ever-useful raincoat, boots for sludging around in the mud or sandpit, a change of clothes, and enough warm clothes to see him or her through the day. You should also pack lunch, or food and drink, since the park attendants or supervisors only act as custodians supervising children at play.

The idea of a *barnepark* is rooted in the belief that a healthy outdoor life leads to a healthy child. Moreover, the park does not need all the infrastructure of a kindergarten, such as classrooms, sleeping rooms, playrooms, toilets, and so on. It consists of a one-room building housing the outdoor playthings – shovels, pails, plastic toys, tricycles, etc. – and a toilet. The enclosed area includes a play area with a sandpit and swings, see-saws and slides, as well as space for cycling or running around. That's it. The bare necessities of life.

In rain or shine, snow or cold, expect your *barnepark* child to be running outdoors. It is all quite healthy, barring the common cold, if your child is well-dressed for the season. Some universities in the cities have a *barnepark* in the vicinity to cater to the needs of their married female staff or students.

The daycare playground is best suited for children between 2 and 5 years old. It is open 4 hours a day in the summer, half the year, and

3 hours in the winter. It is easier to get your child placed in a *barnepark* than in a daycare centre. The former is often operated by women's groups and associations. Contact the daycare playground directly, or the daycare centre office in your municipality. The cost for a place in a *barnepark* varies, but is usually lower than daycare centre rates.

## Barnehage

A *barnehage* translates literally as a 'children's garden' or kindergarten. There are kindergartens run by different organisations such as the municipality or the church. Kindergartens in Norway may be public or private. Opening hours vary from 3 hours to 8–9 hours a day. Some kindergartens have fundamentally different teaching principles and enrolment requirements, so discuss these with the manager of the kindergarten before you enrol your child.

Once you have decided, apply for a place in the kindergarten. The deadline for application (*søknadsfrist*) is normally in the spring, and the actual date is published in the newspapers. (Not all municipalities have a set application deadline.) The application must be written on a special form (*skjema*), which you can obtain from the daycare centres or the daycare centre administration in your municipality. (It may be at a social welfare or school office.) The daycare centre board in each municipality is responsible for allocating places.

Children who enrol in a kindergarten are between 2 and 7 years old. Children normally given first priority are:

- children with disabilities who can benefit from the daycare centre;
- children of single parents;
- children from homes where there is an illness;
- children from a home where both parents are working because of a difficult financial situation;
- children with poor living conditions, or who need a change in their environment;
- children in other situations, which are evaluated on an individual basis.

The fee is approximately NOK1.700–3.500 (US$234–481) per month for one child in a municipal daycare centre. Some private daycare centres require an additional entrance fee. Some municipalities offer a sibling reduction, which means a lower rate applies for brothers and sisters if both are attending a daycare centre. In most municipalities, parents with a very low income can apply for a free place or reduced rates.

Your child should bring food to the kindergarten and be equipped with playclothes, rain attire, and boots or shoes. Most kindergartens have a playtime when children can frolic in the playground in the cities or climb up rocks and grass on the slope behind the kindergarten in the suburbs. If you usually make macaroni or fried rice as a packed lunch, your child will soon educate you. All the children bring sandwiches to school.

## *The Recreation Centre and Full-day School*

Some municipalities provide recreation centres (*fritidshjem*) offering activities and a place to stay before and after school for children in the first three grades of primary school. Some centres provide dinner. Children receive help with their homework and play under adult supervision. You can apply for a place through the daycare centre office or the school office in your municipality.

Instead of a recreation centre, some municipalities offer a 'full-day school' (*heldagsskole*) for children attending the first three grades. The children can be in the full-day school before their school day starts in the morning and after school is finished in the afternoon. They engage in sports, painting, and all sorts of interactive activities. Rates are set by the local authorities. This is a good option if both parents work outside the home.

# *COPING WITH YOUR CHILDREN'S FRIENDS*

Norwegian children make it a habit to visit each other after school, and yours may be invited home with a classmate. Sometimes a classmate may want your child to stay overnight at his or her house.

You may find that some Norwegian parents are very relaxed about letting their children stay overnight at friends' homes. Don't feel pressured to follow Norwegian patterns of behaviour in the district you live in. You should feel comfortable with your decision. If you do not want your child to stay overnight, say so and make sure your child understands your reasons. Norwegian parents will always respect your decision as a parent.

You may find Norwegian children ringing your doorbell to ask if they might visit. Sometimes the children are lonely at home or they simply want company. By all means let them in. You will find that they will come again. Should they drop in at an inconvenient time, tell them so. You need your own time with your children.

Your child may be invited over to a neighbour's house and then be playing outdoors without being invited indoors at all. When you ask your neighbour's child why this is so, you discover that her parents were resting after dinner and did not want to be disturbed by children in the house. At first, you may feel somewhat disturbed by this revelation. When a child is invited to someone's house, you understand that the parents know and welcome it, and the child should be allowed to play indoors as well, not be driven out the moment he or she arrives. This is the way it is in Norway. Norwegians treasure their own private time together and do not think it rude to keep their children's guests outdoors. Your neighbours probably told their child what to expect before your child was allowed to be invited.

## CHILDREN'S DISCIPLINE

Some Norwegian parents are very liberal and others are quite traditionally strict. But bringing up the children is perceived as a collective or joint responsibility, and parents usually agree on the ground rules together. Norwegian children respect their parents. Similarly, parents are supposed to respect their children.

It is forbidden to physically punish children in Norway. Parents who come from cultures with punitive child discipline may find this difficult to understand, but they should observe the law in Norway. Parents, teachers, or other adults who violate this law by smacking, hitting, or hurting a child, whether at home, outside, or in school, can be imprisoned.

There have been some cultural conflicts. In one case, an African immigrant mother had a decorative ring pierced into her daughter's private parts as it was the custom in her tribe. The mother was charged in court as outraged Norwegians rallied around the child, who had tried to resist this custom.

Certainly, cultural misunderstanding and conflict will continue to occur as Norway accepts more immigrants and refugees. The 1993 figures show that 37,550 non-Norwegian children aged 0–19 years reside in Norway. The biggest groups are Pakistani, Danish, and Vietnamese children. These immigrant children form 4% of all young people under 20 in Norway.

## CHILDREN'S ACCIDENTS

Norwegian children are very independent and healthily active. Their parents give them the freedom to be themselves and at the same time, like all parents, exercise parental control and restraint. Despite precautions, children will get hurt. Accidents are the biggest cause of children's health problems in Norway.

About 125,000 children every year are affected by accidents in some way or other. This figure works out to 1 in 6 children per year. And 60–70 children aged 0–14 years die annually in accidents. Accidental deaths account for the largest number of infant deaths. Norway has 37% more fatal accidents among children than Sweden.

About 40% of all children's accidents happen at home, and 50,000 children aged 0–14 years experience some form of home accident every year. The most common causes are:
- falling from heights, e.g. steps, windows, hammocks;
- falling on slippery surfaces;

- cuts and wounds from glass doors, window glass, and kitchen equipment;
- poisoning, especially medicine, cleaning products, and petroleum products; and
- burns.

Be aware of the dangers that threaten your child at home and take preventive action where possible. Accidents also happen at school and on the road, so it is impossible to protect your child totally. However, knowing the risks will make you more careful and appreciative of the care that the country takes with children.

You should also be aware that every clinic or hospital in Norway has a division devoted just to children. Paediatricians and psychologists are around to offer counselling and guidance at the health station or *helsestasjon*. You should feel confident in using these facilities available to you as a parent residing in Norway.

## DRUGS AND SEX AMONG TEENAGERS

Studies done in Norway indicate that there is a strong relationship between the use of tobacco or alcohol and drugs. Half of the teenagers who smoke or drink are apt to experiment with hashish.

If you live in Oslo or Bergen, there are certain districts you would want to avoid after 8 p.m. In Oslo, there is a place in the city square where young people gather to smoke and take drugs. In Bergen, in a park near the university, drug addicts gather in the evening and sometimes harass passers-by for money.

A random study in the Oslo area showed that about one teenager in five has tried hash, and they were introduced to the drug at the age of 13 and 14. Hashish addiction has been described as a gang phenomenon. Teenagers who try out drugs do so primarily because of peer group pressure. If you are a parent with teenage children, discuss this frankly with them.

In 1988 and 1989, 3,000 youths between the ages of 17 and 19 were interviewed about their sexual practices. What is evident from this study is that young people in Norway have a very healthy and positive attitude to sex and sexuality. The average age for their first sexual experience is 18 years for boys and 17.3 years for girls.

## *LEISURE ACTIVITY CLUBS* – **FRITIDSKLUBB**

Schoolchildren in Norway have 50 more free days than their working parents. Many spend their leisure in their immediate surroundings. In summer, many children may go away for their summer vacation to the family home by the sea or in the mountains, or visit other towns and recreation spots in Norway. In autumn, the nights get longer and darker, and children may not know how to entertain themselves.

Norway has this interesting phenomenon of leisure activity clubs (*fritidsklubb*), which are organised by church groups, motivated parents, or the Housewives Association (*Husmorlag*). One-third of teenagers aged 14–16 are members of *fritidsklubb*. Sometimes membership is based on affiliations with sports organisations or other youth clubs. These leisure activity clubs could be located at the old school building or at someone's house.

At the *fritidsklubb*, adult volunteers teach woodwork and hobbycrafts. The children make little objects and take them home to decorate their rooms. Sometimes, the activities in these clubs are geared towards preparing for Christmas and charity bazaars. The atmosphere in the club is cheerful and friendly, and your child could make some good friends there.

## *LET YOUR CHILD PARTICIPATE IN SPORTS*

Norwegian children watch television for about one and a half hours daily. Most of the children's television programmes are in the early evening after dinner. Norwegian censorship of violence on television is quite strict, and children's programmes are educational though not always entertaining. However, with the invasion of satellite television and the multiplicity of channels from around the world, Norwegian children are bombarded with a wide array of choice. On the

*Children testing out a home-made 'hut' in their neighbour's garden. The roof is yet to come on, turfed with grass and ready to be climbed upon.*

whole, however, children in Norway have so many activities to engage their interest, usually outdoors, that they are not much inclined to become couch potatoes. In fact, children watch less television than adults; senior citizens over 70 years are the real addicts.

Many children in Norway participate in organised leisure activities before they are 5 years old. About 94% of 14-year-olds are members of several organisations. They are all engaged in some form of club activity at least once a week. Some join the school orchestra or choir; others are members of a sports club.

Sports is a popular activity in Norway among young and old alike. Parents encourage their children's sports interest. Sports clubs are very popular, and most have sections for different types of sports such as soccer, athletics, swimming, skiing, etc. The clubs are largely organised on a voluntary basis. This means active parent participation in a variety of roles such as administrators, football or soccer coaches, and support groups to ferry the children to competitions.

## *GIVING BIRTH IN NORWAY*

If you happen to get pregnant in Norway, you will discover that a midwife or *jordmor* (literally earth mother) will deliver your baby when the time comes. A doctor will do the first checkup when you suspect you are pregnant. Thereafter, you are in the safe hands of a well-trained midwife.

Regular checkups at the public health clinic (*helsestasjon*) during the entire pregnancy is free. If you are a member of the national insurance (see Chapter 8), your medical consultations and hospital stay will not cost you a cent. In fact, if you do not have work outside the home, you will receive a single payment as a birth benefit from the national insurance.

If you live in the city, your travel to hospital may take 15 minutes or less, but if you live in the countryside, the nearest hospital may be one and a half hours away by car and ferry. Do not cut time too fine. Once you feel labour contractions, especially when it is not your first child you are expecting but the second or third, contact your midwife who will tell you if the signals are reliable indications of impending birth. Thereafter, she will arrange for an ambulance to pick you up. If you are rushing down the mountain with your husband at the wheel, you may meet the ambulance midway up or down the mountain and change your mode of transport. The ambulance will contact the ferry service and the ferry will wait for you to arrive before it sets off across the fjord.

Once you reach the county hospital, you will be wheeled into the delivery room where your familiar midwife will leave you in the care of the midwife on duty at the hospital. After delivery, do not expect to be mollycoddled by Norwegian nurses. Giving birth is seen as a normal process that exacts a slight strain on the new mother, but she is not expected to be helpless.

You might be surprised to find that the attending nurse is not Norwegian but English! Norway is short of nurses and invites professionally trained nurses from the Philippines, England, and other countries to work in the hospitals.

A Norwegian maternity ward is very comfortable and soothing. There is a changing room for babies, and fathers visiting can be alone with their wives and new babies, changing diapers together. The hospital also has a visitors' room, a very pleasant place to entertain family and friends interested in seeing the new baby.

## BRINGING UP CHILDREN IN NORWAY

Bringing up children in Norway is an exciting experience. Children who have never seen much of forests and mountains will find the outdoors a delightful discovery.

When your children are teenagers, there is a little more worry about adaptation in a different cultural milieu and the fear of your children reacting to peer group pressure and following an undesirable crowd. You teeter on a delicate balance between giving your teenagers rights and granting privileges – make sure they know the difference. But certainly, Norway could be a positive influence on your children as they learn independence and responsibility in an environment that encourages a love of nature and a respect of private individual space.

## INFORMATION

Norway is a wonderful oasis of information leaflets and brochures from different government departments. If you want to find out more relating to children, contact the Children and Family Department:

Barne-og Familiedepartmentet
Postboks 8036 Dep
Mollergt 4
0030 Oslo

— *Chapter Six* —

# ART AND CULTURE

Norway has spawned famous musicians like Edvard Grieg, playwrights like Henrik Ibsen, artists like Edvard Munch, and sculptors like Gustav Vigeland. Contemporary Norwegian musicians include saxophonist Jan Garbarek, jazz singer Karin Krog, and jazz bass player Arild Andersen. Norwegians appreciate art and music and celebrate the mass populism of music in street festivals as well as in concert theatres.

Every year, in May, Bergen hosts a major international music festival. Molde, a town known as the City of Roses (because so many roses grow there and adorn balconies and sidewalks), hosts a jazz

172

festival. Jazz and music lovers from different parts of Norway make sure they take their summer holiday in Molde during the month of June when the festival is held. Bergen offers an annual Grieg festival with a series of Grieg concerts in the light and airy Grieghallen (Grieg Hall), itself an architectural delight. Oslo plays host to Ibsen fans every year when it becomes the venue for the Ibsen Festival celebrating the literary achievements of this founding father of modern drama. In Haugesund, an international film festival is one of the highlights of the year. Major international art festivals are held annually.

Culture is very much part and parcel of the people's lives. Norwegians are very proud of their artists, writers, and musicians and today, many younger Norwegians continue their parents' tradition of decorating their walls with art pieces. Nowadays, the trend is to adorn their homes with lithographs and paintings by up-and-coming artists. Norwegians are slowly awakening to the appreciation of art, especially modern art. They are reading about art and artists, and when they buy a piece of art, they usually do so not as an investment but because they like that particular piece.

## NORWEGIAN LITERATURE

A major indoor activity in Norway is reading. Norwegians read more than any other population in the world, spending an average of NOK500 per year per capita on books. More than 2000 new books are published annually in Norway. Around 10% of these are novels, collections of short stories, and books of poetry.

The earliest evidence of literature in Norway are runic inscriptions telling powerful heroic and mythological tales and sagas of kings and families. The stories originated in the Old Norse Period (750–1300). *Heimskringla*, the history of kings, is still a bestseller in Norway.

In the 17th century, the poet-priest Petter Dass ruled the literary scene. The leading figure in the Age of Enlightenment was Ludvig Holberg, who wrote poetry, essays, and comedies of manners. Bergen celebrates this famous son of Norway in a statue that occupies the

173

town square, and every year, a Holberg play is telecast. Henrik Wergeland is another renowned poet, one of the greatest Norway has produced. Wergeland emerged in the years of growing patriotism and national pride preceding Norwegian independence in 1814.

The second half of the 19th century is known as the Golden Age. It was during this time that the Nobel prize-winning Bjørnstjerne Bjørnson and Henrik Ibsen lived and produced their famous works. Knut Hamsun began his writing career around the turn of the century, followed by Sigrid Undset with her novels of women in the early centuries of Norwegian farming life. Both Hamsun and Undset were Nobel prize winners, in 1920 and 1928. Hamsun's *Sult* (Hunger) was made into a movie and Undset's volume on the life of Kristin Lavransdatter is a classic.

Other authors to watch out for are Arne Garborg, Olav Duun, Johan Falkberget, Sigrid Hoel, Tarjei Vesås, and Johan Borgen, as well as the poets Olaf Bull, Herman Wildenvey, Olave Aukrust, and Arnulf Øverland. Not all their works are available in translation.

## Modern Literature

Critics have identified the late 1980s and early 1990s as the era of female authors and an emphasis on social criticism and political radicalisation, rather than on individual psychological studies. The pendulum appears to be swinging back again, for it seems that today more writers are trying to combine the best elements of social criticism and psychological portrayal.

Norway enjoys a rich diversity in literature, not least owing to the official cultural policy. One thousand copies of most Norwegian books of fiction, poetry, and drama are purchased for distribution to libraries around the country. Many writers have also been granted a guaranteed annual income by the government.

Nonetheless, the impact of imported literature is noticed everywhere. You will have no problem in finding the latest international bestsellers.

## IBSEN AND NORWEGIAN THEATRE

Ibsen is undoubtedly the most famous of Norwegian playwrights. At almost any time of the year, at least one of his plays is performed somewhere in Norway. Plays like *Peer Gynt* (the artistic impulse for Grieg's *Peer Gynt Suite*) and *A Doll's House* (identified as the forerunner to women's liberation) are internationally well known.

The most prominent Norwegian dramatist after Ibsen was Nordahl Grieg in the 1930s. Grieg wrote plays dealing with the human psyche and human relations, questioning always the inner soul.

In Europe, Norway acknowledges itself as a very young country as far as theatre traditions are concerned. Professional theatre started as recently as 1827 when Johan Peter Strømberg, a Swede, opened his theatre in Oslo. The National Stage in Bergen is Norway's oldest existing theatre and has been operating continuously since 1876. The concept of a national theatre in Oslo was not realised until 1899.

From the end of the 1970s until the present time, there has been an explosion in the world of theatre and performance art. In the 1960s, the permanent theatres of the big cities – the National Theatre, the Norwegian Theatre, and Oslo New Theatre in Oslo, the National Stage in Bergen, Rogaland Theatre in Stavanger, and Trøndelag Theatre in Trondheim – extended and started several subsidiary theatres, and production of plays doubled.

During the 1970s, five new regional theatres were opened in Tromsø, Molde, Førde, Skien, and Mo i Rana. The regional theatres are based in their respective towns where they rehearse and produce, but during long periods, they tour within their own districts.

The National Travelling Theatre (Riksteatret) was founded in 1948, based on the model of the Swedish Riksteatret. In Norway and Sweden, the sparse population is spread out over a large area, and economic support given to Norwegian theatres is unique. The government, county, and local authorities provide grants covering from 80% to 90% of the expenses involved in running permanent theatres. Norwegians believe that in a small country like Norway, serious theatre activities would be impossible without large contributions to public funding.

Indeed, a visit from the Riksteatret is a treat, especially in the winter when people have time to spare. The performers usually present their act in the local school hall and children are encouraged to attend and be part of the arts scene.

## Free Groups

Free theatrical groups have thrived in the wake of the 'cultural revolution' of the 1960s; they include traditional groups, independent groups, or ensembles that experiment with alternative types of theatre. Free theatre groups have made significant contributions to theatrical activities in Norway in the 1970s, and their first permanent theatre, the Black Box, was opened in Oslo in 1985. Several smaller theatres of a similar kind have opened in Bergen and Trondheim. Free theatres have largely attempted to run decentralisation programmes. But they often have financial problems and far too often end up closing down after a short time.

## SONGS OF NORWAY

In the 1970s, a film entitled *Song of Norway* depicted the life of Edvard Grieg, Norway's national musician. Today, Grieg belongs to the world and his music, ranging from the stately majesty of *Åse's Death* to the whirling intoxication of *In the Hall of the Mountain King*, pleases many. Grieg (1843–1907) is undoubtedly the greatest Norwegian composer of all time. His Piano Concerto in A-minor, Symphony in C-major, and *Peer Gynt Suite* are familiar compositions.

### Grieg and his Frog

For a long time now, the story of Grieg's secret mascot – a 6 centimetre rubber frog – has been going around the music circles. Apparently, Grieg used to keep this 'pet' frog in his pocket and stroke its rough back with his thumb to calm his nerves before a concert.

*A caricature of Edward Grieg, a Norwegian musician of world renown, famous among other things for his* Peer Gynt Suite.

Some say the frog cured Grieg of the intense stage fright he suffered before a performance.

Grieg's frog somehow makes him more human, but it was a secret all his life. It was only when Grieg's wife Nina died in 1935 that the frog and the secret were passed down to one of her woman friends in Denmark. In the late 1980s, the frog was brought back to Norway and is now part of the permanent exhibition at Grieg's home, *Troldhaugen* (Garden of Trolls).

In Grieg's music, you will find fantasy and imagination, power and depth. Here is the soul of Norway. His songs evoke images of towering mountains, snow-capped grace, mysterious peaks, and interior spaces. There is magic and beauty and poetry, and it is for all these reasons that Grieg has become a citizen of the world.

## Music – The Top Brass and All That

During the 1980s, the role of music in Norway underwent dramatic changes. One of the developments is that working conditions for major orchestras in larger cities have improved tremendously with the building of concert halls.

New conductors have revolutionised the size and quality of Norwegian orchestras in recent years. The best known orchestra outside Norway is the Oslo Philharmonic Orchestra. In 1977, the present conductor and artistic director of the Oslo Philharmonic, Mariss Jansons, was appointed. He has led the Oslo Philharmonic to a position among the best in the world. The orchestra is often invited to guest performances in other countries and has made several prize-winning recordings.

The Norwegian Chamber Orchestra has also received considerable international attention. Following a guest performance in Paris, under the musical direction of Iona Brown from the Academy of Saint Martin in the Field, the orchestra was acclaimed as one of the four best chamber orchestras in the world.

Norwegian orchestras are well known for their brass players and this is not surprising considering that Norway has more school bands than any other country in the world. Schoolchildren are encouraged to take up a musical instrument as an extracurricular activity.

Ole Edvard Antonsen is a popular trumpet player today. He is primarily a classical musician but he experiments with other types of music, including jazz, pop, and rock. Pianist Leif Ove Andsnes and cellist Truls Morck are also internationally acclaimed young Norwegian musicians.

If you are a music lover, don't miss Bergen's annual music festival, because this gathering is a good meeting place for musicians from all over the world. Tickets to concerts and theatre performances can cost several hundred kroner.

## *Ole Bull and the Troll*

Arve Tellefsen and his violin are Norwegian classics. The music that Tellefsen spins from his strings sings of farms and fjords, of melancholy and loneliness, of gaiety and happy times.

The violin is a respected instrument in Norway. Outside a main hotel in the centre of Bergen is a statue of Ole Bull, a Bergenite, playing his violin. Legend has it that the magic he played on his strings was so entrancing, a troll who lived in the fjord beneath the water heard it and could not resist rising to the surface to listen more closely to his music. This particular troll was also a musician but he lured innocent people to their deaths with his music. When Ole Bull played his violin, the troll rose out of the water, forgetting the danger of being exposed to the natural air and bright sunlight. The troll turned into stone and so the people were relieved of the terrible curse of his music. It took one great musician to enchant another.

The statue in Bergen has Bull fiddling away and an engaged troll listening attentively to him and turning into stone in the process. The statues, incidentally, are of stone.

## Arne Nordheim

Arne Nordheim was born in 1931 and is one of several renowned contemporary Norwegian composers whose works are played in different parts of the world. A cello concert by Nordheim, commissioned by Mtislav Rostropovitsj, is on the repertoire of many orchestras, and his ballet *The Tempest* is frequently performed.

## Opera and Singing Stars

One aspect of music not appreciated by all is opera. Norway has its share of opera stars, one of whom is soprano Elisabeth Norberg-Schulz, a young singer of significant international repute. She has sung at La Scala in Milan, and was an enormous success when she performed with Luciano Pavarotti at the Viennese National Opera. Her father is another well-known personality: Christian Norberg-Schulz is acknowledged as a writer, an architectural critic, and a historian of world renown.

Soprano Kirsten Flagstad (1895–1962) has been called 'the voice of the century' while Ingrid Bjoner is another prominent singer in the

Strauss-Wagner tradition. Mezzo-soprano Edith Thallaug, tenor Ragnar Ulfung, soprano Marianne Hirsti, and bass baritone Knut Skram are also in great demand. Norwegian opera stars are frequent guests with other European opera companies as there are limited employment prospects for opera singers in Norway.

## A-Ha!

A-Ha is made in Norway and proud of it. This pop group is popular among the teenyboppers in the world and its songs have often made it to the hit charts. A-Ha had its international breakthrough with the single *Take On Me*, in 1985. The group also wrote the title melody for the James Bond film *The Living Daylights*.

Several other Norwegian pop/rock groups like Dum Dum Boys, CC Cowboys, Dance with a Stranger, and September When are popular within Norway. Steinar Albrigtsen and Jonas Fjeld have fans within the fields of country, roots, and pop music.

## Sissel Kyrkjebø, 'Nightingale of Norway'

In the Winter Olympics of 1994, a young woman stood tall and proud and sang the Olympic Song. Her name is Sissel Kyrkjebø. In Norway, Kyrkjebø is a household name and her popularity began when she won a national singing competition as a bright-eyed teenager. Her melodious voice thrills with the splendour of perfection and Norwegians are justifiably proud of her.

## GOVERNMENT SPONSORSHIP

Established cultural activities, including music, are largely financed by the government. However, in more recent years, private sponsorship from leading corporations has become more common. Interest in music has generally increased. Queen Sonja's International Music Competition, arranged for the first time in 1988, is yet another example of the increasing interest in Norwegian music both at home and abroad.

## *NORWEGIAN MOVIES*

The big towns have their own cinema halls but the smaller towns do not, which is why much is made of a trip to the nearest town to watch a movie. In winter, particularly, there is a special feeling that starts with the anticipation of an evening out and then driving through the snow with a couple of friends to watch a good movie, before adjourning for hot cocoa or late-night drinks at someone's house.

Cinema tickets cost around NOK30. There is little of the popcorn and soft drink culture in Norway. When Norwegians go to the movies, it is to see a movie, not to soak in all the informal culture that goes with watching movies. If you are a regular movie-goer from a non-Norwegian culture, you will be glad to miss all that crackling paper and munching noises that go with popcorn and silver wrapping.

Norwegian cinemas offer a wide variety of high-quality foreign films. Few films are produced in Norway. Among memorable films by Norwegian directors are Arne Schouen's *Gategutter* (Street Boys, 1949) and *Ni Liv* (Nine Lives), which was nominated for an Oscar in 1957.

The Norwegian film industry is a fledgling industry. During the first half of the 1980s, it was dominated by female directors such as Vibeke Løkkeberg, Anja Breien, and later, Bente Erichsen. By the mid-1980s, a male phase began with Ola Solum's *Orion's Belt*, an action thriller about the Svalbard Treaty and international politics, and Leidulv Risan's *Etter Rubicon* (After Rubicon, 1987). The high technical quality of these films proved at last that Norwegians were more than capable of making movies geared towards international market and taste.

The late 1980s witnessed international acknowledgement for the Norwegian film industry. Oddvar Einarson's *X* (1986) won the jury's special prize in Venice, a film festival second only to Cannes in prestige. *X* was a simple black-and-white film presenting modern-day Oslo as an emotional bomb-crater.

But the greatest modern success in Norwegian is, without a doubt,

Nils Gaup's debut film *Veiviseren* (The Pathfinder). The story is based on Sami folklore from the Middle Ages, with text from the Sami language. *Veiviseren* received an Oscar nomination for Best Foreign Film and was, against all odds, a great international success, winning excellent reviews from the critics.

Martin Asphaug's *En håndfull tid* (A Handful of Time, 1989), Britt Nesheim's *Frida-med-hjertet in hånden* (Peace with Heart in Hand, 1991), and Erik Gustavson's *Herman* (1991), and *Telegrafisten* (The Telegraphist, 1993) are among the most memorable films made in recent years. *Herman* was about a boy who lost his hair and *Telegrafisten* is an evocative and sensuous film about passions and desire.

Nils Gaup also experienced international success with his adventure film *Håkon Håkonsen*, in 1991. There were two versions – English and Norwegian – of the movie, which starred a Norwegian boy in the lead role and an Englishman in the other protagonist role. This movie had mass appeal because of its shipwreck and adventure theme. *Døden på Oslo S* (Death in the Underground, 1991) played to packed houses in Norway while *Giftige Løgner* (Poisonous Lies, 1992) was another box-office hit.

## NORWEGIAN ARCHITECTURE

A Norwegian's house is his hearth and his sanctuary. It is the place where he can feel at home. Norwegians are a house-proud people, and perhaps this can be explained by cultural aesthetics.

According to Christian Norberg-Schulz, 'In our divided, microstructured landscape, it isn't natural to gather settlements in large units where together we can meet life. Instead, we dream back to each hill with each small lake or brook. Likewise, we own these surroundings together and they have given us a deep common identity. ... Flickering hearths over rose-painted walls conjure forth again the trolls and giants. Thus lives the Norwegian and thus he shows that he is friends with the Norwegian nature.'

Norberg-Schulz's book *Mellom Jord og Himmel* (Between Earth and Sky) explores the history and guiding principles of Norwegian architecture and identifies the stave church, of which 30 remain, only in Norway, as the finest expression of wooden architecture. No nails are used in the construction of the stave church which has withstood the ravages of wind and weather for 800–900 years. Norway is the only country in which wooden church architecture was developed to such an extent that medieval churches could be preserved up to the present time. The best known of the remaining stave churches is probably Borgund Stave Church, built about 900 years ago.

Building with wood is a characteristic of Norwegian architecture. A few large-scale stone complexes were built, including military fortifications (such as Akershus Fortress in Oslo) and the important and splendid cathedral in Trondheim where stone craftsmen created a building comparable to some of the finest examples in France and England. But wood has remained the national building material. It was only in the 19th century that there was a need for new buildings in materials other than wood – primarily in stone.

In the beginning, the architects supervising the construction of these new projects were foreigners. Subsequently, they were replaced by Norwegians who were primarily educated in Germany. The most successful of this period is the old University in Oslo, built according to the drawings of Christian H. Grosch (1801–65) and completed in collaboration with the great German architect K.F. Schinkel. Towards the end of the 19th century, there was a national trend towards architecture in wood. This resulted in the distinctive dragon style inspired by the secular log houses and stave churches of the Middle Ages.

Henrik Bull's transformation of the international Art Nouveau style just after the turn of the 19th century also reflects national inspiration. The Classicism of the 1920s and the Functionalism of the 1930s both gained a foothold in Norway as well.

Postwar architecture after 1945 was initiated by the numerous

*Heddal Stave Church is a good example of a well preserved stave church, although not so well known as Borgund Stave Church.*

construction works. German occupation had left the entire northern part of the country totally burnt down. Rapid economic development took off, resulting in mass development of housing areas, industrial estates, and commercial buildings. This architectural period embodied a pragmatic, no-nonsense form of architecture.

As the country prospered, increasingly more effort went into the quality of its built physical environment. However, some small towns and rural areas lacked planning experience, leading to what some writers have called 'prairie development' – with commercial buildings and not much regional context. There is now a growing concern about how this situation can be improved, and some counties have started publicity campaigns and advisory programmes focussing on the architecture and planning of small towns and village centres.

A number of Norwegian architects have won international acclaim. These include Arne Korsmo from the early postwar period. Later, Geir Grung and Sverre Fehn designed a number of single houses, as well as institutional developments such as the exhibition hall at the splendid Maihaugen outdoor folklore museum in Lillehammer. Fehn, who is still active, is probably the best-known Norwegian architect today. Among his latest works is the glacier museum in Fjaerland on the west coast of Norway.

Lund og Slåtto, a Norwegian architectural firm, has designed churches, housing areas, institutional buildings, and offices that have been presented in many international journals. Architects such as Niels Torp and Snøhetta have won recent major international competitions. The latter won UNESCO's competition for the Alexandra Library complex in Egypt. Torp's works include Aker Brygge, a redevelopment of Oslo's seafront, SAS (Scandinavian Airlines) headquarters in Stockholm, and British Airways headquarters near London. His firm was one of the architects for the Hamar Olympic Hall, also known as the Viking Ship, in Lillehammer, site of the 1994 Winter Olympics. Norwegian architects today are international, yet there is still a quest for a national, uniquely Norwegian style.

## DAHL AND MUNCH

Before Edvard Munch, there was J.C. Dahl (1788–1857), who became a professor in Dresden. Dahl's paintings of Norwegian landscapes won him a prominent position among his contemporaries. Munch followed after, winning international recognition with his expressive works of the interior landscape of the mind and soul. Munch's work influenced German art of the 1910s and 1920s. A pioneer in the development of the graphic arts as an independent art form, Munch is represented in museum collections all over the world.

In later years, monumental paintings were produced in Norway that had an impact on other Nordic countries. This culminated in the ornamentation of the Oslo Town Hall by Per Krogh (1889–1965) and other artists. Climbing the Town Hall steps is a visual and aesthetic experience. Today, some of the leading names in Norwegian painting are Jakob Weidemann, an abstract painter whose works are often inspired by nature, Franz Widerberg, a figurative expressionist, and Per Kleiva, almost a pop artist. Of the younger generation of painters, Odd Nerdrum is a representative of Neo-Romanticism.

## SCULPTURE AND OSLO'S VIGELAND PARK

In June 1993, Oslo's Vigeland Park was officially declared open, 50 years after the death of its namesake and initiator. The ceremony involved the unveiling of Vigeland's sculpted self-portrait, which became part of the park's collection of outdoor exhibits. The Vigeland Park is one of Norway's biggest tourist attractions and draws one million visitors a year. If you live in Norway, visiting this park is an eye-opener to Norwegian art and sculpture.

Gustav Vigeland (1869–1943) was the first Norwegian sculptor to win international renown. His sculptures in Vigeland Park depict the various phases of man, from infancy through adolescence to maturity and old age. They rivet the eye with their attention to detail and the consummate skill with which they have been executed. Vigeland's *Angry Boy* throwing a tantrum reminds many a parent of irate children in a difficult situation, while his larger-than-life sculptures of man and woman are simple and erotic at the same time. The park's crowning masterpiece is a totem pole of figures clambering up, child upon man upon woman, interlinked in fate and destiny.

The pioneer of abstract sculpture in Norway was Arnold Haugeland (1920–83), who was given a number of official commissions. The figurative tradition is carried on by Nils Ås, while Boge Berg exceeds the traditions of traditional figurative sculpture. Among the younger sculptors, Gitte Daehlin has gained a following among Norwegians with her textile sculptures.

## ARTS AND CRAFTS IN THE HOME

Norwegians do not believe that art and history have a place only in museums. Their sense of historical continuity is very much present in their homes where grandmother's weaving loom occupies a quiet but central place in the sitting room and handwoven rugs or 'runners' grace the floors of living and dining rooms. If Norwegians have a display cabinet, you will find old silver mugs and other small handicraft on display. The embroidered tablecloth that decorates their dinner table might have been inherited from their mother. The wooden decorative spoons on the walls might have been crafted during a course at the local handicraft group.

The Arts and Crafts Association or *Husflidslaget* is gaining popularity in Norway as Norwegians who are interested in handicraft flock to the various courses designed to teach them how to produce their own *rosmaling* masterpieces or handwoven table runners. *Rosmaling* is a distinctive Norwegian art whereby special oil paints are used to produce graceful designs of flowers and leaves that have a flowing line and fine colours of gentle hues.

The local *Husflidslag* usually organises summer courses, but Norwegian handicraft enthusiasts also enrol in the courses organised by the district Handicraft Association, which runs special schools in rustic surroundings for this purpose.

*Local handicrafts at the county fair – complete with spinning loom and a long-haired white rabbit to provide the wool!*

Handweaving is now a popular pastime among Norwegian women. In rural Norway, some women have been creative enough to recognise the uniqueness of homespun wool. These women raise their own long-haired rabbits (a particular breed with very long hair that can be snipped off and spun into wool) and take them to the local fair where they demonstrate with ease and confidence the art of spinning from long hair.

Knitting is another very popular pastime. Many Norwegians wear handknitted woollen sweaters or caps in winter. Since clothing can be an expensive commodity (the mail order catalogue is a popular alternative to shopping in the mall), Norwegians have turned to knitting their own clothes. At the same time, knitting has always enjoyed a fine tradition in Norway. Women do it in winter before the fireplace in the sitting room, or while watching television or chatting with friends over a cup of coffee. Some men indulge in knitting as well. Norwegian sweaters are well known for their original designs and motifs, and a handknit sweater always makes a thoughtful gift.

Norway has a long tradition of wood-carving. Magnus Berg (1666–1739) had an international reputation as a carver of ivory, but there is ample evidence of Norwegians' wood-carving skill – from Viking art and the ornamentation of stave churches to the highly developed folk ornamentation that exists today.

The art of weaving is also well developed in Norway. A leading weaver of the day is Synnøve Aurdal, who uses new materials such as metal and plastic in her tapestries. Norwegian pottery finds expression in the outstanding works of Kari Christensen while jewellery design by artistes like Tone Vigeland bears the distinctive traits of Norwegian quality.

## NORWEGIAN CULTURAL POLICY

Official Norwegian cultural policy is based on a concept of culture that embraces not only the preservation of art and culture, but active participation and individual initiative. Cultural activities in Norway are mainly financed by the public sector and cultural councils exist in almost all counties and municipalities. In addition, the Norwegian artists' associations are the only organisations of their kind with negotiating rights. It is also typical of Norway that institutions receiving considerable government support are run by the artists themselves.

# Chapter Seven

# DOING BUSINESS
# AND
# WORKING IN NORWAY

Honest. Reliable. Trustworthy. These qualities seem to describe Norwegian business people best. When you are in Norway to wrap up or initiate a business contract, you will find your Norwegian counterparts seated at the table, prepared to do business with a focused determination and little allowance for distraction. They are direct and go straight to the point, wasting little time for interaction other than what is necessary for the immediate business at hand. Your transaction is given instant attention. There is little attempt to break the ice.

Sometimes this directness can work to their disadvantage, especially when they negotiate with people from other cultures who expect a degree of harmonising in a light buzz of conversation before the actual discussion of a contract. Norwegian straightforwardness can be rather disconcerting.

## *LET'S GO STRAIGHT TO THE POINT*

Norwegians believe in the distinct separation of work and play. When you do business, you talk business. You do not indulge in personal queries about family or other matters. The usual negotiating structure that begins with exploration, leading up to bidding and bargaining, and culminating in settling and ratifying is usually not followed by Norwegians in business.

Generally, the Norwegian is more cautious than other Scandinavians in business, for example, the Swedes. Norwegians are trustworthy but distrust others at the negotiating table, notably foreigners. They expect, to a certain degree, that others will operate on the same principle they adhere to – namely get the business done.

It's been said that Norwegians are more linear in their pattern of transaction than other people. What this means is that Norwegians are more prone to see things in one perspective. There is no practised manoeuvre in hedging or sidestepping. They are more confrontational about issues. They forget that sometimes the walk up the garden path can pave the way for more successful negotiation. The house is still at the end of the path; it can wait.

Some people have tried to explain this Norwegian propensity for directness in their business exchange as a trait of their ancestry. Norwegians perhaps are still traders rather than marketeers, they say. There is a certain rigidity, an eye on short-term profits, with little sophistication in the art of contact-gaining for future references. Norwegians have not sufficiently learnt the important skill of selling themselves abroad, of presenting themselves on the international scene as credible business partners who are out to win a competitive edge. There is a certain casualness about Norwegians in business that some identify as a lack of the competitive spirit.

## *PUNCTUALITY*

Norwegians are generally punctual people. If they say 3 o'clock, they mean 3 o'clock. Especially if you are doing business with Norwegians, make sure you are on time. There is no stretching of time, no rubber time. There is, however, what is known as the academic quarter. What this means is that your Norwegian host will allow you a grace period of 15 minutes. After that, you are in disgrace.

The idea of punctuality applies to working hours as well. Most Norwegians prefer to leave the office on the dot. There is a story of how a foreign businessman was speaking on the telephone with a Norwegian counterpart when he was suddenly interrupted by her gasp of realisation that it was already 4 o'clock. "Gosh, it's 4 o'clock!" she said, and promptly hung up. This, naturally, is an extreme example.

## *THE NORWEGIAN WORK ETHIC*

The goal of most Norwegians, some foreigners believe, is to work as few hours as necessary in order to get off to the mountains, away from people, or to engage in sports like skiing or hiking.

Norwegians are responsible workers. They work hard and diligently in the office, but they also jealously guard their private time and space, and the opportunities for enjoying the open spaces that are their right. Norwegians will leave punctually from the office and seldom bring work home, unless it is vitally necessary. If there is great urgency, they will work overtime. But they would much rather not.

Plan your meeting schedules well. The fact that you have limited time in their country may not convince Norwegians to bend their principle of keeping leisure time their own.

## *DO NOT COME BEARING GIFTS*

Do not approach business with the idea of influencing your Norwegian partner's mind with the presentation of a gift. Such an action will alienate you and leave the Norwegian feeling most suspicious and cautious. He or she will begin to question the implications of your action. Even if you have the best of intentions and bringing a gift reflects your cultural upbringing, avoid making your Norwegian business acquaintance feel awkward and uncomfortable; gifts are only for special occasions like birthdays and Confirmation.

Perhaps such honesty is antiquated, but at least you know where you stand with a Norwegian. There is no insidious innuendo or suggestion. On the other hand, Norwegians may be considered rather naive in the business world because they do not analyse underlying motives and tend to accept statements at face value.

## MAKING SMALL TALK WITH A NORWEGIAN

If you ever get the chance to make small talk with your Norwegian business acquaintance, you are lucky. If you have discussed business already and are relaxing over coffee, you will find that a Norwegian's art of conversation is limited to outdoor life and sports, two activities they love and thrive on. Do not enquire too closely about their family – how many children they have, what their husband or wife does, etc. – they will think you especially nosey. Just mention the Winter Olympics, skiing, or hiking, and they will loosen up in no time at all.

You will find that Norwegians understand quite a bit of what you say in English. But beware that they have not missed the implications of an idea you are trying to convey. Sometimes, Norwegians are loath to admit they have not understood all the details rattled off in English. They grasp the general idea, but that may not be good enough for you. To avoid frustration, always check to see if your Norwegian business counterpart has understood the fine print of a business conversation.

To encourage Norwegian business friends to relax completely, a Canadian businessman has suggested breaking the ice with a cocktail party before business negotiations are opened. Norwegians enjoy good alcohol, and can get quite friendly when suitably warmed by fine wines. This might not be a bad idea, since it would be clear to everyone that such interaction is primarily and obviously social, apparently with no hidden motives.

## *DO NOT BARGAIN WITH A NORWEGIAN*

Norwegians can be inflexible. If the specifications they present to you are not to your satisfaction and you ask for amendments and changes, you might meet with some resistance. "This is the way we have been doing it all these years. It was good enough then. Why is it not good enough for you now?" Or "Why is it not good enough for you when it is good enough for others?"

Norwegians can also be stubborn. "This is our price and that's it." No budging. No quantity discounts. Negotiating with Norwegians is usually in either black or white; there is no grey area. This makes some foreign business people think that Norwegians are tough customers.

Those more used to a gradual and cautious opening up of their business contacts may find Norwegians' directness confrontational and feel somewhat threatened by the immediate presentation of their intentions. Norwegians lay their cards on the table immediately whereas some may hold back to see what game the others will play.

However, the international competitive environment is changing the way business is done in Norway. Norwegian management has in many areas been isolated from foreign currents of thought, the result of Norway's raw material industrial base. But this is changing as the country develops its competitivenss in finished consumer goods.

## *ALWAYS DELIVER WHAT YOU PROMISE*

Never promise Norwegians something you may not be able to deliver. Say only what you can be sure of, not what you hope to do. Norwegians always expect you to keep your word. *They* do, so why shouldn't you? Make empty promises and you will lose their trust.

Norwegians appreciate honesty and sincerity more than fine words. Once you have gained their trust, you have it forever. In dealing with Norwegians, you have to learn patience, be well-prepared and documented, and have your facts at hand. Any promise is regarded as binding so be careful what you want to say before you open your mouth.

## *ACCESSIBILITY AND OPENNESS*

If there is one phenomenon in Norway that will surprise and please you, it is the degree of openness. Accessibility is seldom hampered by individuals and organisations. Most people will try to satisfy your curiosity for more knowledge and clarification. The media is able to get the information it wants. Immigrants are able to find out what they are entitled to and how they can improve themselves. Everyone has the right of access to anything in Norway.

This accessibility applies also to getting in touch with important people. If you want to make an appointment with the chairman of an organisation, chances are you will be put through to him directly by his secretary on your first enquiry. This is a great liberty to people who have known the frustration of having themselves and their telephone calls filtered by diligent and protective secretaries. You will appreciate not having to go through the drill of revealing every detail of what you want to say to their superiors before you gain access to them.

Norwegians are not overwhelmed by titles and name-throwing. You might find Norwegians rather casual about your title or even royalty. Impress them instead with your personality and actions.

## *A FISHBOWL MENTALITY*

Norwegians in business can be guilty of a narrow parochialism, which makes them imagine that what they know is best. The idea that 'Norway is the best' is part and parcel of Norwegian nationalism. Norwegians are proud of their country and their achievements. Some sociologists have said they have an image of how the world ought to be – and one in particular (Johan Galtung, *Norwegian Society*, 1974) says 'that image requires first and foremost that the world be a larger edition of Norway'.

## *THE BOSS DOES NOT DECIDE; WE DO*

Norwegians are said to be in no hurry to rush things in business. They tend to pay a great deal of attention to details, and this can be an admirable quality. They do not commit themselves to an agreement easily. First, they will discuss, then examine the details, then they must discuss again. Decision-making can take time because in Norway people believe in consensus. Caution is another reason. Norwegians weigh the alternatives and forget perhaps to make the decisions.

Many people may be involved in the decision-making process. Approval sometimes has to come all the way from the floor. The floor decides and the boss affixes his or her signature. Critics have commented that Norwegians seem to exhibit a horde mentality that affects their management style.

## PEER GYNT AND THE NATIONAL CHARACTER

Henrik Ibsen, the great Norwegian playwright, wrote a famous play that was embraced by Norwegians as a national play. The play was *Peer Gynt* and the young man in the story was content with fantasy and evaded reality. The name Peer is the Norwegian equivalent of the English Peter, a common name for Everyman. Peer Gynt was identified as a representative Norwegian.

In his book *The Norwegian Way of Life* (1954), eminent Norwegian lawyer and writer Frede Castberg claimed that Norwegians lacked self-confidence. Their humility or apparent downplaying of their self-importance could, however, be paradoxically an expression of a subtle form of national boastfulness. Castberg noticed a tendency in the Norwegian to vacillate, to show 'uncertainty and self-criticism, side by side with all his self-assertiveness and self-satisfaction'.

This quality is alleged to be present also in Peer Gynt, and is attributable to the extreme contrasts in Norwegian topography and weather. In Norwegian, it is identified as *tvisynet* (self-doubt).

## A DIMINISHED SPIRIT OF COMPETITION

The idea of Norwegians being naive and laid-back in business, with no great desire to win that contract by any means except their own notions, seems to be supported by a lack of ambition.

Some sociologists believe that success and achievement are not major preoccupations in their life because they grow up feeling secure and protected. There is no sense of struggle or a desire to compete at work, nor to excel except in sports. Perhaps Norwegians are given a sense of omnipotence too early in their childhood by their parents. The Norwegian child is not required to excel in order to win a parent's approval. The child is left to grow up in an environment that promotes a sense of self-sufficiency and independence.

This characteristic is also enforced by the physical conditions of Norwegian landscape and climate. Castberg once said that 'Everywhere people are separated by fjord and mountain and sea, and in that way every mind becomes a separate kingdom, all on its own.'

## A FREE SPIRIT

Norwegians are very proud of their independence and their relative self-sufficiency. Social anthropologist Eduardo Archetti, who has lived in Norway for many years, observes that Norwegians generally dislike having to feel indebted to anyone. They seem to be afraid of upsetting the delicate balance in their relationship with others. For example, they prefer to buy cigarettes from strangers instead of asking them for a cigarette and accepting it. They won't let anyone pay for a cup of coffee without reimbursing them at once. A favour must be returned immediately. The length of time that elapses between giving and getting back is absolutely crucial.

Norwegians apparently consider short-term exchanges to be the best way of keeping track of how much passes between two people. According to Archetti, this makes it possible to avoid inflation as well as deflation. Everyone knows what they owe each other at any given time. It is more difficult to keep track of long-term exchanges and there is a greater chance of upsetting the balance. Archetti believes this Norwegian characteristic springs from a deep-rooted belief that reciprocity is directly related to independence. The individual should not organise his life so that he becomes a burden to others.

## WORKING IN NORWAY

It is important to familiarise yourself with Norway's current laws and regulations. And the first rule is that all foreigners, except nationals from other Nordic countries (Denmark, Iceland, Finland, and Sweden), must have a work permit in order to work in Norway.

### Wages

If you are employed in Norway, you should think about opening a wage account (*lønnskonto*). Your salary is then paid directly into your bank account by your employer. This is the normal practice in Norway. Being an established client of the bank will be an advantage if, for example, you apply for a housing loan.

When your salary is paid, you will receive a wage slip or notice (*lønnsslipp*) containing information about your gross earnings and deductions that have been made. You should try to be systematic about keeping these wage slips. Tax is always deducted in accordance with the scale on your tax card (*skattekort*) when your wages are paid. This means that your take-home pay every month is less this tax deduction. At the same time, you may be deducted for tax previously due, or for child contributions (*barnebidrag*). Your employer does not have the right to deduct other expenses, such as rent or meal allowances, unless a written agreement exists to this effect.

### Working Hours

Workers in Norway work up to nine hours daily and up to 40 hours a week, i.e., an average of eight hours a day, five days a week. Shift workers have a shorter working week of 36 to 38 hours.

The start of the working day varies from one job to another. Most offices begin at 8 a.m. and finish at 4 p.m. Others begin at 7 a.m. or even 9 a.m., and close eight hours later. The working hours of shops correspond to their opening hours. Many work places now practise flexible hours – employees start work later and work correspondingly later in the evening, or the opposite – but there are fixed basic hours (*kjernetid*) when everyone has to be present. In many offices, you may have to clock in and out. All public and private offices work a five-day week.

If you work more than 40 hours a week, the excess hours are considered to be overtime hours. You have a right to at least 40% overtime pay when you are obliged to work overtime. However, in top positions, and if you are self-employed, you will not normally have a legal right to overtime pay.

Everyone working more than $5^1/2$ hours daily has a right to a meal break (*spisepause*). If the working day lasts more than 8 hours, meal breaks must total at least 30 minutes. In some places, breaks are considered part of the 'working hours'.

Each week, you have a right to at least 36 hours of continuous free time. According to the regulations, you should have at least 10 hours free between working shifts unless another agreement exists that has been approved by the Labour Inspectorate. If you work at a place where it is not possible to have weekends free, such as a hotel or hospital, the free day must be on a Sunday or public holiday every second or third week.

If you are a mother breastfeeding your child, you have the right to work one hour less than normal each day. You may choose whether to come later or leave earlier, or whether you prefer a break in the course of the day. If you are employed part-time, you also have the right to shorter working hours in order to breastfeed your child.

## *Holidays*

Adult employees have, according to the law, the right to four weeks plus one day holiday each year, totalling 25 weekdays plus the intervening weekends. This applies even though you may work fewer than five days a week. Employees aged 60 and above may have five weeks plus an extra day.

In 1990, a new Holidays Act stipulated that the period upon which holidays are based is from 1 January until 13 December. You have the right to three weeks' holiday during the period from 1 June to 30 September, although your employer may decide when you can take your holiday between those dates.

You can have a written agreement with your employer that up to 12 days' holiday can be transferred to the next holiday year, or that the whole or part of the holiday is taken in advance. There are no specific regulations concerning leave of absence without pay before or after the holiday period. It is up to your employer to grant any application for leave without pay.

In Norway, you also get extra money when you take your holiday. This is in addition to full-paid leave. All employees have the right to holiday pay (*feriepenger*). This is about 10% of the salary earned during the previous year. Persons over 60 years receive about 12.5%. Holiday pay is paid when you take your holiday. If you leave a job, you receive the holiday money together with your final wages.

Norwegians respect the religious holidays of other religions besides Christianity. Employees who are members of a religious faith outside the Church of Norway have the right to two free days each year in connection with religious celebrations, but your employer can require that you work a corresponding number of days at another time.

If you are ill for at least six days during your holiday, you have the right to take a corresponding number of days' vacation later. You must have a doctor's certificate and make your claim as soon as you return to work.

## *Sick Pay*

If you are ill and unable to go to work, you should immediately inform your employer on the first day you are ill. This is important in order to receive sickness benefit from the first day. Ring your employer, or ask someone else to do this for you. You may be ill for up to three days and inform the employer yourself, but if you are ill for more than three days, you must have a doctor's certificate. If you are ill on a Friday, then the Saturday and Sunday are also considered sickness days. You can declare yourself sick up to four times a year, but in order to receive sick pay, you must have been employed at least two months before you make a self-declaration.

The first two weeks you are ill, your employer is responsible for your pay. After this, the social security system is responsible. Sick pay, with certain exceptions, will correspond to your normal salary, and tax is paid in the normal way. The social security office in your locality can give you more information.

If you are responsible for the care of one or more children under the age of ten, you have the right to time off when the child is ill. The general rule is that you have the right to up to ten days off work for this reason, during a calendar year. You can use the self-declaration in the case of your child's illness for up to three days at a time. After this, you must have a doctor's certificate if your child is ill.

## STARTING YOUR OWN BUSINESS

If you are starting your own business, the type of firm to establish will be one of the first decisions you will make. The establishment of a smaller firm will either incorporate a private enterprise or a limited (share) company (*aksjeselskap* – A/S).

You might consider several options, for example a one-man enterprise, a joint enterprise (*ansvarlig selskap* – ANS), or a limited company (A/S) with limited responsibilities. Guidelines including share capital required and obligations are outlined in a brochure (in Norwegian) entitled *Formelle krav ved foretaksetableringer i Norge*. It gives information on the various types of companies and the formal requirements, and is published by the Department of Trade (*Naeringsdepartementet*).

### Getting a Business Licence

In order to start a business, such as a shop, you must be an adult above 18 years of age. You must not have been declared a bankrupt, you should be resident in Norway, and have lived here for at least the last two years. The Department of Trade may, however, waive the residential conditions in special circumstances.

In addition to the normal work permit, foreigners must have special permission from the police to conduct business, and this approval will be entered in your passport. Application forms for self-employment are obtainable from the local police. To start a shop, you must register with the Company Register (*Foretaksregisteret*) in Brønnøysund. This is a register of all companies conducting trade. If the firm does not trade with purchased products and does not have more than five employees, it need not be registered.

Applications to the Company Register is made on a standard form obtained from *Foretaksregisteret*; different forms exist for different types of company. The form must be signed by the proprietor or person responsible for the company, and the signatures must be confirmed by a lawyer or two other adults. Both *Foretaksregisteret* and the Ministry of Trade can supply further information. There is a registration fee, the amount depending on the type of company.

It is also necessary to inform the following if you start a shop or other type of firm:

- The tax office (*Ligningskontoret*) will issue a tax card and calculate prepaid taxes and social insurance;
- The county tax office (*Fylkesskattekontoret*) will provide a special registration form if you start a firm that is obliged to pay value-added taxes (*moms*), or if you take over an existing firm. You must inform the county tax office in order to be registered as liable for value-added tax. Turnover must exceed NOK12.000 in any year.
- The social security office (*Trygdekontoret*) must be informed of all employees so that they can be registered in the sickness benefit fund;
- The Directorate of Labour Inspection (*Arbeidstilsynet*) must be informed as soon as a firm starts operations or changes address.

For businesses without a fixed locality, the regulations are less stringent. This form of business must be registered with the County

Governor (*fylkesmann*). For certain types of trade such as secondhand business, permission must be obtained from the police. Permission for other types of business such as market or street sales are given by the local authority regulating this type of trade.

## Starting a Restaurant

If you are interested in starting a restaurant or a guest house serving refreshments, apply to the local authority for a licence. The health authorities must approve the locality. If you wish to start a restaurant serving alcohol, you must also apply for a licence. The right to serve alcohol (*skjenkerett*) is granted to the individual establishment. In Oslo, application is made directly to *Restaurant-og beuillingskontoret*. Elsewhere, you should apply directly to the local authority where the premises are located.

It is also necessary to obtain a licence to operate transportation vehicles, such as taxis, ambulances, and cars for hire. The County Communications Committee (*Samferdselutvalget*) in each county grants these licences.

## Keep Your Accounts Straight

Everyone operating a business or firm must keep accounts. The law distinguishes between complete and partial accounts. Complete accounts must be kept where the trade is engaged in purchased products. This implies a complete inventory of trade and an annual trade balance. All expenses and income must be carefully documented. The accounts and receipts should be retained for at least 10 years. Contact the Banking, Insurance and Securities Commission (*Kredittilsynet*) for more information.

## Getting a Grant to Start a Business

In Norway, a special fund exists for those wishing to establish a firm, in particular in a rural area where the economy is weak. The Norwegian Industrial and Development Fund (SND), as it is presently organised, started its activities on 1 January 1993. Its main purpose is to promote the profitable commercial and socio-economic development of the Norwegian economy in all parts of the country. The SND contributes towards product development and the establishment of new enterprises and assists in the development, modernisation, and restructuring of Norwegian business and industry.

The SND supports, in particular, measures that can lead to long-term, profitable employment in regions where the economic base is weak. The instruments that SND has at its disposal include loans, guarantees, grants, and equity investments.

Application for assistance is made to your nearest SND regional office, the SND Head Office in Oslo, or the department of economic development in the County Office (*Fylkeskommunen, naeringsavde-lingen*), in the county where you intend to establish the business. The county is responsible for processing SND's regional development measures. In the case of equity investments, the county administration will evaluate your proposal before referring it to SND's Venture Capital Division.

## *Establishment Grants*

Because of increasing unemployment, grants have been made to individuals in recent years to establish new and permanent work places. The grants are not restricted and may be applied for anywhere in Norway. Anyone may apply for a grant for projects in any occupational branch, except those within public service and the primary industries (forestry, agriculture, fishing, etc.).

These establishment grants (called *etablererstipend*) are designed for unemployed persons, women, and those wishing to start a firm in areas with employment problems. Each project is carefully evaluated, and the business opportunities it brings is considered in the decision to award a grant.

The grant, which may be awarded during the development phase, or as a subsidy for starting a business, is subject to tax. Up to

NOK200.000 may be granted, and advice and information are given during the establishment period. The application should be made to *Naeringsavdelingen* in the County Council; in Oslo, apply to *Veiledningstjenesten* (TI). The address of the latter is:

Teknologisk Institutt (TI),
Veiledningstjenesten,
Akersv. 24 C,
Postboks 2608 St. Hanshaugen
0131 Oslo.

## OTHER KINDS OF SUPPORT

A support arrangement exists for grocery shops in rural areas where very few people live and the survival of the shop is questionable. Support may be given for building or expansion, modernisation of the premises and stockroom, necessary equipment, and operational costs. Support is not given in order to establish a shop, only to existing businesses. The Department of Trade gives support in the form of grants to the county. Application can be made to the Office of Trade in the county.

The Industrial and Regional Development Fund (SND) may give support to those wishing to start a business in industry or travel. You must have a solid business concept and be able to answer questions concerning the profitability and development prospects of the project or enterprise. The Fund gives priority to enterprises within the travel industry that are aimed at tourists.

The Research Council of Norway (NFR) has its own fund for 'Innovations in Business'. Different types of support are given to projects whose aim is business activity, especially that based on advanced technology and the results of research.

## PAYING YOUR TAXES – SKATT

In Norway, taxation has two purposes: to cover the expenses of society, and to reduce the differential between the highest and lowest incomes. This is brought about by imposing progressively higher taxes with higher income levels. Taxes pay for medical assistance, childcare, pensions, and education, as well as for communications, highways, and other community services. Norway offers its residents many free services but its taxes are among the highest in Europe.

Income tax is also used to subsidise certain essential goods and services, so that the consumer pays a price lower than the cost of production.

## *Direct and Indirect Taxes*

Income tax and wealth tax (on things owned, such as a house, a car, or bank deposits) are direct taxes. Taxes are paid to the local authority (*kommune*), county (*fylke*), and the state. In addition, a premium is paid to the social security system that enables you to receive free hospital and medical treatment, as well as contributes to old age pensions, disability pensions, and unemployment benefits.

The most important indirect tax is value-added tax – VAT (*moms* or MVA). This is a 22% tax applied to most goods and services. All self-employed persons have a duty to apply this tax to sales of goods and services, and it is a punishable offence to evade this tax in Norway. The chief county tax inspector will supply more information on value-added tax. Certain articles such as cosmetics, cigarettes, and alcohol are subject to special state taxes. If you live in Norway for a period of less than six months, special tax regulations apply. To find out more, contact the local taxation office.

# Chapter Eight

# SOCIAL SERVICES AND ISSUES

The special feature about the Norwegian health service system is that health services are financed through compulsory membership in the national insurance scheme. The scheme, which will be referred to often in this chapter, covers the entire population and has its own budget, which is adopted each year, along with the fiscal budget. An important principle of the scheme is decentralisation of responsibility. In practice, this means that the municipalities and county municipalities plan and operate the health services.

In addition to health institutions, county municipalities are responsible for specialised medical services outside institutions, child welfare, institutions for alcoholics, and laboratory and X-ray services. In 1991, the county municipalities relinquished the responsibility of health care for the mentally retarded to the municipalities.

Most municipalities provide housing for pensioners and transportation for the disabled. Home nursing and house-help facilities are included. If you need help with housework because you are old or handicapped, for example, or because you are undergoing pressure at work and cannot cope with domestic chores, you can contact the social welfare office and ask for house help. All you have to do is state the period you require the service and pay the rates charged. If you request it, the house helper will also cook meals for your children.

The objective of Norwegian social services is to prevent social problems, promote economic and social security, and improve living conditions for the individual. A further aim is to enable as many people as possible to be self-sufficient and to lead an active and meaningful life with others. The municipalities have the central role in implementing current social policies.

The task of the state is to define national goals and draw up the framework of conditions for the health service, provide advice and guidelines, and supervise the health service in the municipalities and county municipalities. The state is also directly responsible for a number of institutions with national functions, such as the National Hospital and the Norwegian Radium Hospital in Oslo.

Health expenditure constitutes about 14% of total public expenditure. The cost-sharing charge – the cost that must be covered by the patient, and which is not refunded by the state – amounts to roughly 10–15% of the total costs of the health sector.

Protective measures have been introduced to ensure that users of health services are not financially overburdened. In 1984, an arrangement was initiated whereby no patient is to pay more than NOK880 a year in health expenses. The state reimburses payments on consultations with doctors and psychiatrists, essential medication, and necessary travel if these expenses together exceed NOK880 per year.

## *NATIONAL INSURANCE –* **FOLKETRYGDEN**

Norway is a welfare state and two main social insurance schemes exist that embrace the general population and families: the national insurance (social security) scheme and the family allowance scheme. Anyone residing or working in Norway is insured under the former.

This means that if you are working in Norway, you are covered under the national insurance scheme, unless you are a paid employee of a foreign state or an international organisation, or receive insurance coverage according to foreign law. You are considered to be resident in Norway if you are living in Norway for more than one year and your residence permit is in order. Even if you do not have a job, you are entitled to health services.

If you have refugee status, you are entitled to all types of benefits even if you have not previously been a member of the national insurance programme, and even if you have just arrived in Norway. The rules for refugees apply for as long as you live in Norway. If you are seeking asylum, you have a limited entitlement to social security benefits (including entitlement to some health services) until your application is decided.

## *CHILDREN'S PENSION*

A child under 18 is entitled to a children's pension if one or both parents are deceased and one of the parents had been able to work and was insured with entitlement to pension benefits for one year immediately prior to death. The child is also entitled to benefits if one of the parents had been drawing a pension for at least one year prior to death. Children still studying receive the pension until 20 years of age if both parents are deceased. There are special rules if one or both parents died as a result of work injury.

### *Adopted Children and Other Special Cases*

Adopted children are entitled to a child pension upon the death of an adoptive parent. However, foster children and stepchildren are not entitled to a child pension. Children of a deceased immigrant can receive a pension from the national insurance, even if they do not live in Norway. The conditions are that the deceased must have lived in Norway for at least three years and the child is only entitled to the pension if he moves to Norway.

Norwegian society has embraced many homeless orphans into its midst through adoption. In Norway, you may find a neighbour down the road coming home with a newly adopted baby or preparing to collect the new baby in Korea. Childlessness is usually the main reason for adoption, but sometimes the motivation is compassion and love for the deprived and homeless. You can find Norwegians who adopt victims of war because they sympathise with their plight.

In 1991, there were 833 adoptions in Norway. Adoptions within Norway has remained stable over the years, but the statistics for adoption of foreign children has risen from 498 in 1983 to 562 in 1991. There is a slight difference in the ages of adopted children. Most of the adopted foreign children are below 3 years old while adopted Norwegian children are often over 3 years old when they are adopted.

Two-thirds of adoptions in 1991 concerned foreign children. South America, with a large proportion from Colombia, ranks highest, followed by Asia, where at least half come from Korea. Adoptive parents are married couples and adopted children often have older adoptive parents than their Norwegian counterparts.

## CHILD SUPPORT – BARNETRYGD

Child support is the economic support the state gives all in Norway who are bringing up children under 16 years of age. The child support law of 1946 upholds the principle of financial allotment to parents, especially mothers, and the amount corresponds with the number of children in the family. *Barnetrygd* is a financial buffer for parents.

Only children who have lived in Norway for more than 12 months are entitled to the child benefit. Children who stayed in Norway for less than 12 months are not considered to be resident there. The child benefit is paid from the month following the birth of the child and continues until the month the child turns 16 years of age.

This allowance ensures that the person who has the daily care of a child receives a minimum amount of money for necessary expenses. It is paid to the child's mother unless the father has the sole care of the child. If you happen to have the sole care of a child or of children, you are entitled to one more child benefit than the number of children you are caring for.

You can claim your child benefit no earlier than 30 days after the birth of your child. The person who has the care of the child must contact the social security office (*trygdekontor*) in the municipality and report the birth.

## CHILD WELFARE – BARNEVERNET

The child welfare authorities in each municipality keep a close eye on the living conditions of children and young people under 18 years of age, and help them if they are living in undesirable social conditions.

Child welfare officers may visit homes where there are problems and give help and advice. Assistance can also consist of helping to place a child in a daycare or recreation centre, helping the child get into a school or get a job, or helping to find the family a support person or financial assistance. Anyone who is aware of children who are in such straits has a duty to report to the child welfare authorities.

## ATTENDING TO A SICK CHILD

When your child is sick and you are working, you are allowed to seek a maximum of 10 days' leave a year to tend to your child's illness. If your child is sick, you get full pay for the days you are absent from work, but you will not be compensated if you have to take leave because your childminder is sick and you have to look after your child yourself. Single parents have an additional 10 days' leave in this case.

Terminally ill children are entitled to have their parents by their side for a year. Employers must pay the parents full pay for this year.

## *DAILY BENEFITS*

These cover various categories of people and conditions.

### *Sickness Benefits*

A person covered by the national insurance scheme is entitled to daily cash benefits if incapable of work due to sickness. As a general rule, the person should have been working for at least 14 days. Conditions are attached, including a certain basic annual income.

### *Maternity Benefits*

An insured woman who has been working for 6 out of the 10 months preceding confinement is entitled to daily cash benefits for 165 days or 33 weeks. If the mother resumes work before the period of paid maternity leave has lapsed, the father is entitled to the daily cash benefits for the remaining period if he stays at home to care for the child. A woman not entitled to daily cash benefits in the case of maternity receives a maternity grant.

Working women who give birth are entitled to a year's maternity leave. The first 6 weeks of postnatal leave are taken by the mother and the remaining 46 weeks can be taken by either parent. The mother can also choose to take 12 weeks of prenatal maternity leave. Fathers have the right to ask for 2 weeks of no-pay paternity leave. About 80% of fathers in Norway take advantage of this scheme.

New mothers have a good deal in Norway. From 1 April 1992, mothers were entitled to up to 33 weeks of maternity leave with full pay (*fødselspenger*) or 42 weeks of leave with 80% of the normal salary. The requirement is that the mother must have been professionally employed for at least 6 of the 10 months before the birth of her child. The same rights extend to foreigners working in Norway.

### *Unemployment Benefits*

All those who have had a job and received a certain minimum income before they became unemployed have a right to a daily allowance from the national insurance scheme. To receive this, they must apply at the state employment exchanges found in all towns and major municipalities.

Receiving unemployment insurance is conditional: among other things, the applicant must regularly register as a work-seeker at the employment exchange and is under obligation to accept the work offered. The unemployed has a right to a daily allowance for a period of 80 weeks. Thereafter, if still unemployed, the daily allowance is withheld for 13 weeks. During this period, economic support can be claimed through the Social Care Act. A daily-rated supplement is also given for each dependent child under the age of 18, and this is increased after 26 weeks' unemployment.

## OLD AGE PENSION

In Norway, the average life span is 80 years for women and 74 years for men. The pension age is 67, although some special occupations have a lower pension age. The retirement age in Norway is 70. There are no provisions for early retirement under the national insurance scheme, but the old age pension may be wholly or partially deferred until the age of 70.

Those who have been members of the national insurance scheme for 3 years and are at least 67 years old receive an old-age pension regardless of whether they have had paid employment. Those who continue to work in full employment are not paid an old-age pension. Those who earn less than before can receive a partial pension. The old-age pension consists of a basic pension, a supplementary pension or a special supplement, and possible supplements for children and spouse.

At the age of 70, you receive a full pension even if you still have an income from work. The lowest full old-age pension you can receive through national insurance is called the minimum pension. Spouses who are both pensioners do not get double the amount, but a reduced figure.

A supplementary pension scheme was introduced in 1967 to prevent a marked decline in the standard of living upon retirement. The supplementary pension amount depends on the number of years worked. A full supplementary pension requires 40 pension-earning years. For fewer years, the pension is reduced proportionately.

## FUNERAL GRANT

In the case of death, a lump sum grant is given by the national insurance scheme to cover funeral expenses.

## MARRIAGE AND THE FAMILY

The average Norwegian family comprises the father, mother, and one or two children. Only a few families have more than three children.

In the old days, grandparents stayed with their children and grandchildren, but today, many couples and their families are nuclear units. Even on the farms, there is a tradition that the son or daughter who inherits the farm lives in the main house while the parents move out into a much smaller cottage. In the cities and elsewhere, the majority of young people reside with their parents until they have completed schooling, often around the age of 19 or 20. It is also common for a teenager to leave home at 16 to study at a college in another town. Norwegian children are used to being independent.

### Tying the Knot

Marriage can take place in a church or a civil ceremony which is performed by a justice of the peace (*borgerlig vigselsmann*), city recorder (*byfogd*), or district recorder (*sorenskriver*). You must provide a best man and a bridesmaid who know you well. They must be at least 18 years old and have to testify to the fact that the bride and groom are not closely related and that neither of you is already married. The pastor or justice of the peace will inform the Population Register Office (*Folkeregister*) of the marriage and the couple is given a marriage certificate.

If you choose to live together without getting married, you can avoid such formalities. But both partners must be at least 18 years old. Incidentally, when two people from different countries want to marry, it is important to find out which country's rules apply in marriage, divorce, the citizenship of children of the marriage, and other matters. The rules are not the same in all countries and a marriage entered into in Norway is not always valid in another country.

## Property Rights in Marriage

In Norwegian law, when two people get married, they automatically have joint ownership of all their material goods. Unless another agreement is made, the spouses jointly own everything each owned at the time of marriage and everything they subsequently obtain during the marriage.

Spouses can write a marriage contract (*ektepakt*) in which they agree upon complete separate ownership – that is, property or valuables owned by a spouse before entering into marriage, or purchased later with his or her own money, are that individual's own separate property. If the marriage is dissolved, each spouse keeps possession of his or her own property. It is also possible to make agreements concerning partial separate ownership.

A marriage contract must be in writing and be signed by both spouses and two witnesses. The contract is valid with regard to other persons, such as heirs and creditors, only when it is registered with the Register of Mortgages and Moveable Property in Brønnøysund and is written on a special form that can be purchased at a bookshop. If the contract includes real estate, it must be registered at the office of the district recorder or city magistrate's court (*byrett*) or city registrar (*byskriver*). The act of judicial registration is significant if creditors and other inheritors want to make a claim upon the property of a deceased partner in marriage. Even with the contract, the debt will not be honoured by the surviving spouse if no claim is registered officially with the city or district registrar within a certain period of time.

## COHABITATION

Cohabitation is quite the norm in Norway, and cohabiting couples are said to be *samboer* (cohabitants). Cohabitation is like marriage without the paper, especially when children are involved. Fidelity in emotional, physical, and spiritual aspects exists, as in a harmonious marital relationship. Nearly 15% of children under 3 years old have parents who are cohabitants. Norwegian law has adapted to answer the needs of cohabiting couples in terms of property division, custodial rights of children, and other related issues.

Cohabitants have no legal obligations to each other. It is therefore advisable to make special agreements, preferably with the help of a lawyer, concerning property and the custody of children in case of a separation. Cohabitants who have children together do not automatically have joint custody of them. According to the law, the mother has the sole responsibility, but the parents can agree upon joint custody or to give the father sole custody. The Population Register in your municipality must be informed of special agreements. Cohabitants cannot inherit from one another, but they can write a will or testament to each other's advantage. They are taxed separately.

## HOMOSEXUALITY

Homosexual or lesbian bondings have been officially acknowledged, and from 1993, such couples can be registered as 'partners'. They cannot marry but their registered partnership is as good a legal bond as any marital status. One thing partners cannot do is adopt a child, since children of a tender and impressionable age are believed to need parents of both sexes to be role models.

It is punishable by law to discriminate against homosexuals in print or verbally, and homosexuals are entitled to the same social security and public benefits as others. The Norwegian Association of 1948 is a Norwegian association for homosexuals and bisexuals. The association works to achieve understanding for the situation of homosexuals and bisexuals, and protects them from unjust treatment.

## DIVORCE

In 1993, the divorce law was relaxed in Norway. It now takes only one year (if both partners want the divorce), instead of the earlier two years, of separation before a couple can file for divorce. The aim of a separation is to give spouses enough time to reflect on their situation before embarking on the final step.

Before separation, the couple must attend an arbitration meeting. The arbitrator can be a member of the municipal conciliation board, a pastor, or another person approved by the county governor. After arbitration, they receive a certificate of arbitration that must accompany the application for separation and, later, for divorce.

If both spouses agree to a divorce, the period of separation is one year. If only one wants the divorce, it is two years. If the spouses still wish to be divorced after the separation, they must apply for a divorce to the county governor in the county where one or both of the spouses live. The application form is available at the social welfare office (*sosialkontor*) in the municipality or at the county governor's office.

A separated couple no longer has joint finances. But a spouse may claim financial support from the other if he or she has worked only at home for many years. The spouse who does not have custody of the children must help to pay for their care in proportion to financial ability. Those who do not pay the support as ordered by law may find the amount deducted from their wages.

Annulment of a marriage is not common in Norway. A marriage can be annulled in a few cases: for example, if the couple was unaware that they were close relatives, if one of them has committed bigamy, or if one of them had a serious venereal disease without informing the partner before the marriage.

When two people decide to divorce and cannot agree on issues concerning children or property, they can seek counsel with the Family Affairs Office, a lawyer, or the county governor. The Family Affairs Office is run by the local authorities, the county, or the parish. Its function is to solve family conflicts and arbitrate in marriage cases.

217

## SINGLE PARENTHOOD

In 1993, one out of five families were single-parent families, and nine out of ten single parents were mothers. The biggest number of such parents reside in Oslo and north Norway. There are about 110,000 single-parent families in Norway with children below 18 years.

If you are a foreign national who has been granted a residence permit in Norway on the basis of your marriage to a Norwegian citizen, or to another foreign national with a residence or work permit in Norway, the renewal of the residence permit will, as a rule, depend on the continuation of the marriage or cohabitation. You must also still be living together as a couple. However, even if the relationship has ceased, the residence permit can be renewed when one of the following conditions exists:

- if you have children under 18 years of age in Norway, have custody of the children, and fulfil this right; or
- if you are a woman with some ties to Norway who, because of the breakup in the relationship, will experience unfair difficulties in your native country owing to the social or cultural conditions there; or
- if you are a woman who has broken out of a relationship because you or any of your children have been abused.

### Social Security for Single Parents

If you are a divorced, separated, or unmarried parent, you are entitled to benefits intended to help single parents through a difficult transition period. Conditions for these benefits are that you live in Norway and have lived in Norway for the last three years, and that you have the sole care of the child. Entitlement to these benefits ceases if you marry or live together with the father of the child. Financial support can be given till the child is 10 years old.

The social security benefits given are:

- a transition benefit to live on when you cannot hold a job because you are caring for small children;

- an education benefit if you need education or training in order to provide for yourself and your children;
- a child-minding benefit if you are working or studying outside the home;
- a baby bonus for purchasing necessary equipment in connection with the birth of your child; and
- grants and loans for various purposes, for example, moving house or starting up your own business if it is necessary to start working.

If you have your own income, the transition benefit will be reduced. You are not entitled to this benefit if your income exceeds a predetermined level (approximately NOK150.000).

## *NORWEGIAN WOMEN*

Norwegian women seem to have a good deal of equality, more than what some women have in other countries. Norway has an equal rights law, a female prime minister, a government in which 9 out of 19 ministers are women, and an Equal Status ombudsman who tries to ensure that men and women are treated equally in the employment market.

Women have made significant advances in politics. In 1965, there were only 12 female representatives in the Storting, but in the parliamentary election of 1989 women received 59 of the 165 seats. Today, the Storting's president is a woman, Kirsti Kolle Grøndahl. Gro Harlem Brundtland became the first woman prime minister in the history of Norway in February 1981. Interrupted by different conservative cabinets, she has served as prime minister from May 1986 to October 1989, and from November 1990. Anne Inger Lahnstein has taken charge of the somewhat traditionalist agrarian Centre Party where two-thirds of the members are men.

It is obvious that women are at the forefront of Norwegian politics and are active in the agenda-setting process. This is so despite the fact that there are only 29 women mayors, as opposed to 449 men, and three women county governors.

## The Female Voter

In Norwegian elections, votes are cast by choosing a party list, where the party chooses the order in which candidates appear. In local elections, however, voters can influence the order of the candidates. By crossing out the male candidates on the lists, voters can ensure that more women than men are among a party's representatives elected to local government. Slightly over half the Norwegian population are women. Women in Norway got the general right to vote and be elected in 1913, 15 years after Norwegian men got the franchise.

## Women's Rights in Norway

The high proportion of female representation in politics did not happen by accident. Persistent and systematic efforts by women in the women's movement, in the political parties, and in public administration have been rewarded by enhanced female participation in all sectors of Norwegian life. Campaigns were directed towards the political parties as well as the electorate to nominate and elect more women. In addition, the use of quotas was introduced in the political parties' own recruitment and election procedures, as well as in appointment procedures to public committees, councils, and boards.

As early as 1854, Norwegian women acquired inheritance rights. But it was not until the 1890s that married women gained the right to dispose of their own wealth. The Allodial Act (*Odelsrett*) was changed in 1974, giving the eldest child – not the eldest *boy* as in the earlier act – first priority in inheriting a farm. This law resulted in the enrolment of more female students in schools of agriculture as they grappled with the responsibilities of farm management.

In 1882, women were given access to higher education, but it was only in 1903 that the first Norwegian woman received a doctorate. The first female professor came on the scene in 1912. In 1885, a women's suffrage organisation was created, a year after the founding of the first women's rights association, the Norwegian Association for the Rights of Women.

Women can make themselves heard through two channels of representation:

- participation in elections, thereby influencing the composition of the democratically elected political agencies, such as the municipal councils, the county councils, and the Storting; and

- the corporate channel, mostly on the national level, through approximately 1200 permanent and ad hoc committees, boards, and councils. The corporate bodies, especially on the labour and management sides, participate in decision-making or advisory administrative agencies, official boards, and committees, and in this way take part in formulating the content of political decisions. Women's organisations may be represented in these committees, boards, and councils.

Theoretically, there are no sex barriers. Norwegian women can advance on par with men. Equal rights legislation even demands that employers try to recruit more women further up the managerial ladder. The law states that where one of the sexes is strongly under-represented in an organisation, this sex is to be preferred when new appointments are made, so long as the applicants have equal qualifications. Naturally, there is still a gender-divided labour market in Norway, linked to the fact that many women have traditionally chosen to educate themselves within the caring professions such as public health and social welfare, whereas more men have acquired economic or technical skills.

## The Quota System in Politics

The rapid increase of women in Norwegian politics is to a considerable extent due to the quota system. The Liberal Party was the first, in 1973, together with the Leftwing Socialist Party, to opt for the system of having no less than 40% women at the various levels, and no more than 60% of any of the sexes anywhere in the party. The Norwegian Labour Party followed the same example, and attracted worldwide attention in 1986 when the principle of 40% representation was applied also in the Cabinet. At that time, 44% (8 out of 18) of the ministers, including the prime minister, were women.

Competition among the parties has served the cause of women. Even the non-socialist parties, which have been resisting the quota system, have increased their representation of women considerably. Women constitute roughly 40% of the total membership in political parties.

## Women's Organisations

If you are a woman relocating to Norway, you might like to join one of the following women's organisations.

The Norwegian Women's Public Health Organisation (*Norske Kvinners Sanitetsforening*) was founded in 1896 and is today the largest organisation of women, with approximately 240,000 members. It runs about 600 institutions including hospitals, nurses' training schools, kindergartens, and maternity homes.

The Norwegian Housewives' Association (*Norges Husmorforbund*), established in 1915, is the second largest women's organisation. It pioneered efforts to build and maintain kindergartens and other projects for the benefit of children, and to provide assistance for households in emergencies, education through study groups, and other activities.

The Norwegian Country Women's Association (*Norges Bondekvinnelag*), also one of the larger women's organisations, engages in matters related to the vocational status of women in farming. The Norwegian Housewives' Association and the Norwegian Country Women's Association are affiliated to the Associated Country Women of the World, ACWW.

The National Council of Women in Norway (*Norske Kvinners Nasjonalråd*) was established in 1904, and was meant to be an umbrella organisation, open to all kinds of women's organisations. More than 20 organisations were members. It soon became clear, however, that women with socialist leanings refused to join. It played an important role through international contacts, but was dissolved in 1990.

The Norwegian Association for the Rights of Women (*Norsk Kvinnesaksforening*) was established in 1884 to promote the interests of women. Its goal is to work for equal rights and responsibilities for women and men in all spheres of society. It is a small organisation, with about 1000 members, but has served as a leader in the work for the rights of women in education and economic life. Internationally, it is affiliated to the International Alliance of Women (IAW).

The Norwegian Women's Association (*Norsk Kvinneforbund*) is a more radical women's rights organisation, established in 1945. Its target is a socialist society as a basis for the liberation of women. Special attention is given to the need for peace, disarmament, and paid work for women. Its international affiliation is with the Association of Democratic Women of the World.

Working-class women have mainly been organised in female groups of trade unions, or in women's groups of the Labour Party, to protect their interests as wage earners. Today, women constitute about 30% of the 750,000 individual members of the Federation of Trade Unions.

## *Public Equal Status Agencies*

In the 1970s, Norway witnessed the steady building up of a public machinery whose function was to promote equal status and to improve the situation for women in various areas of society. While in 1967, the Ministry of Local Government and Labour appointed women consultants to coordinate and initiate measures concerning women and employment, today, every region has its own 'equality consultant'.

The Equal Status Council (*Likestillingsrådet*) was established in 1972, replacing the Equal Pay Council (1959–72). Its task is to 'work for equal status in all sectors of society, family life, working life, education, and the community in general'. The council operates as an independent consultative body for the government, as a contact and cooperative body between the government, women's organisations, and the public in matters concerning equal rights, and as a deliberating body. The council's seven members are appointed by the government. Both sexes and all parts of the country are represented. Two seats are reserved for the Norwegian Federation of Trade Unions and the Confederation of Norwegian Business and Industry.

In 1977, a Department for Family Affairs and Equal Status was established in the Ministry of Consumer Affairs and Government Administration (now Ministry of Family and Consumer Affairs). The task of the department is to coordinate government policies in matters concerning equal status.

Also in 1977, the Norwegian Research Council for Science and the Humanities (NAVF) established a Secretariat for Women and Research. The secretariat operates within the fields of the natural sciences, social sciences, medicine, and the humanities. Its aims are to increase the number of women engaged in research and to coordinate and promote research on women.

In March 1977, the ministry directed municipalities to set up equal status committees, appointed on a political basis with the same rights and status as other committees in the municipality. By January 1990, 355 out of 448 municipalities (79%) had established equal status committees. In addition, all the 18 counties have established such committees. The Equal Status Council serves as an advisory body for the equal status committees in counties and municipalities.

On 15 March 1979, the Norwegian Equal Status Act came into force in Norway. Its objective is to promote equal status between the sexes and particularly to improve the situation of women, facilitate equality of status between the sexes in all sectors of society, and give equal opportunities for men and women in education, employment, and cultural and professional advancement.

The Equal Status Act is enforced by the Equal Status ombudsman, and is instrumental in maintaining the view that numerical equality is important for equal status. (In 1987, a new rule was introduced which required equal representation for both sexes on public committees and boards. Where this is impossible, as, for example, where the committee has an uneven number of members, a 60-40 rule applies. In other words, there should never be less than a 40% representation of women on a public board or committee. The only exemption from this rule is when there are not enough qualified candidates of a given sex.)

In 1981, the Ministry of Church and Education established a Secretariat for Equal Opportunities in Education. The secretariat has arranged courses for teachers at all levels, presented a framework plan for equal opportunities in teacher education, stimulated the writing of new textbooks, and motivated women to apply for leading positions in schools.

In 1986, the Ministry of Family and Consumer Affairs established a provisional committee to discuss the role of men. It was rightly perceived that without a change in men's role and a sharing of responsibilities for household work and childcare, there will not be equal status between men and women.

## Women in Literature and Sports

Norway has had its share of literary activists who have taken up the fight for equality with their pens. Sigrid Undset, who won the Nobel Prize for Literature in 1928, impressed with her evocative description of women and their realities in her novels set in the Middle Ages. Her most famous work is *Kristin Lavransdatter*. But perhaps the first female novelist to depict women's role in society was Camilla Collett, with her novel *The Governor's Daughter* in 1855.

It is interesting that one male writer was particularly active in advocating women's rights. Henrik Ibsen's dramas featured strong female characters in leading roles, who expressed their need for freedom and emancipation in different ways. *Hedda Gabler* and *The Doll's House* are perhaps his best-known works.

In sports, one woman's name stands out. Grete Waitz is a Norwegian who has won international recognition and acclaim in the marathon race. Each year, the streets of Oslo are filled one Saturday in May with 20,000–30,000 female joggers. Among the crowd is the marathon queen herself, Grete Waitz. She runs with the women to encourage them to complete a 5 km stretch in a race that allows for wholehearted participation and no competition, unless it is perhaps competition within oneself. Waitz's athletic achievements have made her a role model for aspiring sportswomen and encouraged female participation in competitive sports.

# CONCLUSION

'When the spring sun shines on hill and dale, then I do not know a more beautiful country.' This was the general theme among Norwegian national poets and painters in the mid-19th century. The song reflects Norway and its people. The winter can be long and cold. But when spring comes, nature suddenly springs to life. The landscape coloured in winter garb suddenly, within a few weeks, takes a summer gaiety and vitality. Nature and the landscape are transformed. Spring comes, and soon it is summer.

As nature springs to life, so too do the people. Norwegians in summer are somewhat different from Norwegians in winter. They become more outgoing. Social life takes off. The lifestyle pattern changes too. People become less reserved, more relaxed and neighbourly (in the social sense).

Norway is by any international standard a homogeneous society. Yet there are distinguishable regional differences, a result of geography, history, and economic development. The Sami people, although a very small minority, constitute an important and distinct component of the Norwegian culture. New immigrants bring along the culture of their countries.

The Norwegian poet Kolbein Falkeid has written a poem contrasting the nomad and the farmer. One longs to visit new, unknown places, while the other builds his house and tills his fields, reluctant to move. Both of them have left their mark on Norwegian history.

Norwegians live in a beautiful country. They have achieved one of the highest standards of living in the world. They know this. The quest now is for the best ways to improve the quality of life – how to bring about a balance between work and the range of cultural, sports, and other activities which enrich life. How can Norwegians find a happy balance between economic growth and protection of the environment, between retaining and developing Norwegian culture and institutions in the face of other international commercial cultures and mass communications? How can they bring up their children well in a world of changing perceptions and expectations, and at the same time impart to them a vital sense of history, culture, and purpose? How can Norway keep its egalitarian democratic values in a competitive world?

The challenge to Norway is how to sustain the present standard of living and improve the quality of life in the face of growing international economic competition where development in Norway is such an integral part of the larger world.

Today, Norwegians too are experiencing a culture shock of sorts, with the dissolution of national boundaries and the migration of different cultures and influences. But Norwegians ultimately have an inner strength, a resilience that is inbuilt and part of their national cultural heritage. Their sense of inner equilibrium and balance, the result of a tradition of living harmoniously with nature and with each other, will stand them in good stead in the face of change. This, then, is the Norwegian way of life: facing up to, overcoming, and hopefully, coming to terms with different conditions, both in nature and the world of men.

# CULTURAL QUIZ

## SITUATION 1

You and your husband are invited to dinner with the teacher of your daughter whom you consider also to be a friend. She also happens to be your next-door neighbour. Dinner is at 7 p.m. Just prior to leaving for dinner, your teenaged daughter and you have a fallout. She screams, you scream, and it is 7.30 p.m. when you suddenly realise that you were supposed to be at dinner half an hour ago. Outside it is snowing and the road is as slippery as ice. Your neighbour has not called to ask why you are not over, and you are emotionally unprepared for a night out. What do you do?

A  You call your neighbour friend up and tell her you are very sorry. You forgot the time because you had a tiff with your daughter and ask if it is too late to back off from the dinner as you feel so upset.

B  You and your husband go directly to your neighbour's house with the box of chocolates you had bought for the occasion, and when she opens the door to you, you give her the chocolates, kiss her on the cheek lightly and apologise for your lateness, explaining the situation briefly.

C  You ask your husband to go alone – you are simply too torn up to go out to dinner and make small talk. You instruct your husband to make up an excuse, perhaps say you were mugged on the way, and the next thing you knew, you were on the ice, your leg twisted beneath you.

D  You and your husband go to dinner together. You apologise profusely for your lateness, trying to excuse yourself by saying that in your culture, it is customary to come to dinner half an hour late. You do not mention your fight with your daughter at all but pretend everything is fine.

## Comments

*A* would be perceived by your Norwegian hostess as inconsiderate and rude, unless you know her very well and can be frank with her. She has taken trouble with the dinner, and the food has already probably been keeping warm too long. She has laid out her best crystal and porcelain. She has not rung you to enquire why you are late or if you have forgotten because Norwegians really believe their guests know how to keep time. In a normal situation, where you know your hostess only moderately well, you should honour your dinner engagement.

*C* requires your husband to try for an Oscar in his portrayal of a distressed husband. It is dishonest and you must remember that Norwegians are basically upright and honest, and expect their friends to be so too. *C* is going to lead to more than a make-believe broken leg! Your relationship with your neighbour might also be broken, especially when she insists on coming to visit you after dinner with a portion of her special dessert. What are you going to do then?

*D* is what a foreigner from a different culture concerned with saving face might do. In the attempt to avoid washing dirty linen in public, you pretend everything is as it should be. The result is that you may be distracted and upset during the dinner and not do justice to the meal and the hospitality of your hostess, and she, on her part, might feel her dinner was not up to your expectations. She might be astute enough to perceive that everything is not all right. Remember that she might be understanding and offer some valuable advice. Norwegians are usually caring over children.

*B* is the best bet. You are meeting your dinner engagement, albeit a little late. But you explain to your hostess briefly at the door and she accepts your explanation. Later, inside the house, you might discuss the domestic conflict with your friend. In this context, she is hostess first, friend and adviser second. You should acknowledge the priority of her roles and accord her due respect as a hostess. Not many Norwegians invite visitors to dinner at home, especially in winter, so you should be thankful for the invitation and go to dinner.

## *SITUATION 2*

You are in Norway for a business meeting, at the invitation of your Norwegian contacts. You arrive in Norway on Thursday, the terms of agreement are discussed, and you sign the contract on Friday afternoon. You are booked on a flight home on Monday morning. You expect your Norwegian hosts to at least invite you out for a meal on Friday and hope that they will show you around town sometime during the weekend. (They know it is your first visit to Norway.) But evening approaches and the office is set to close, and you see your Norwegian counterparts getting ready to go home. There is no sign of any invitation to dinner or anywhere else. What do you do?

A You ask your Norwegian hosts smilingly, 'Well now that we have wrapped up the contract, what about a few drinks and a meal to relax and get to know each other?'

B You observe them looking at their watches, increasing shock and disappointment registering in your eyes. You can't believe it. It is only 4 p.m. and these people are going straight home. You voice your disbelief. And you mention, with a loud hint in your voice, 'You know, I have never seen a Norwegian home. What is it like? Where do you live? And do you have a garden?' etc. You hope they will take the hint and maybe invite you home.

C  You mention that in your culture, most business meetings usually end up with dinner and drinks. And you wonder what the custom is like in Norway. You leave it at that and play it by ear.

D  You say jovially, 'Well, it is still early yet. What about a karaoke club or a bar? And where do I find places to eat? What should I do during the weekend? Where do you suggest I could go? Hey! Don't tell me you are going home to the family now. What early birds you are! Come on. Let's go out. Come on. Let me buy you dinner.'

## *Comments*

*A* is very reasonable but it exposes you to rebuff and disappointment when your Norwegian counterpart says, 'No thank you. We have to go home.' It is the weekend and the family is waiting. For Norwegians, weekends are a very precious family time. If the Norwegian is a single person, then he or she might accept your invitation and go out for the evening with you. Otherwise, do not expect a Norwegian to volunteer to give up personal time to go out with a business client. The deal has been concluded. Business has been done. Time to go home.

*B* is too obvious. Norwegians are not so dense that they cannot recognise a blatant attempt to invite yourself to their homes. If they liked you enough and wanted to show you their homes, they would have invited you themselves. Nothing you do will change their minds. Playing on guilt or responsibilities of the host party will get you nowhere. Norwegians firmly separate work from play; there is a time for each activity. And they will definitely not rise to your bait if you use *B* as a strategy to manipulate yourself into a Norwegian home.

*C* is again very reasonable and preferable to *A* because it leaves the question of invitation open. *A* closes the door but *C* leaves room for possibility. *C* is a means of culture-sharing. At the same time, you are reminding the Norwegians of their responsibility as hosts and asking for clarification if you have been mistaken in your understanding that they will play hosts to you this weekend. This way, you are making them aware of some of your expectations but not forcing their hand. If they feel conscience-stricken about their lack of hospitality, they will explain that in Norway business is business in the office and weekends are for the family. They might add that they understand your expectation and throw in a dinner invitation or maybe even a visit to their homes – usually they will check with their spouses first.

*D* is being too pushy. You can guess that the Norwegians want to go home, but you want them to go out with you, even if you are going to pick up the tab. Norwegians are relatively mild people, but once they have made up their minds, they won't budge. And no degree of enticement is going to change their decision. So save your breath and ask for a possible itinerary of interesting places to visit over the weekend. They will gladly provide this information.

## SITUATION 3

You are the mother of a teenaged daughter who happens to be a healthy, attractive young woman. You know the boys at her school are interested in dating her. Currently, she seems to be going steady with this apparently engaging young Norwegian called Frederick. (You know Frederick's parents. Your husband is his father's colleague.) You have talked with her about the pleasures and risks of going steady or being intimate at that tender age of 16. She tells you that many of her girlfriends at school think nothing of sex – it is all quite normal and everyone does it. You caution her.

At 6:30 one morning, you walk into the sitting room and who should you see but Frederick, passing you from the opposite direction, where the staircase to your daughter's bedroom is! You ask what he is doing in your house at that unearthly hour. Looking you in the eye, he tells you he climbed up the balcony to her bedroom last night and spent the night with her. Now he is going home. What do you do?

A Your face turns red as a tomato with the shock of Frederick's announcement and you go into an apoplectic fit. You point an accusing finger at Frederick, screeching, 'Seducer! Rapist! Ingrate! Get out of my house. I never want to see you again. Is this how you repay my hospitality? I'll report you to the police. I'll make sure you don't climb up another balcony again!'

B You are terribly shocked and upset at the implication of Frederick's words. You think the worst but have to confirm your suspicions before accusing Frederick who is looking at you with his innocent blue eyes. You want to go upstairs to talk with your daughter. But first, you tell Frederick to go home quite composedly, adding 'Your parents will wonder where you are, Frederick.' Once Frederick leaves, you bolt upstairs and ask your daughter for details of her night visitor who played Romeo on the balcony.

C You are so angry and upset you cannot think straight. You call for your daughter to come downstairs; you scream hysterically for your husband. You call up Frederick's parents on the phone immediately and confront them with what Frederick has told you. You insist on making a lot of noise and ask Frederick's parents to come instantly for a family pow-wow about this crisis.

D You look at Frederick coolly and ask what he did in your daughter's bedroom in the night. You decide it might be a long story and invite him to the kitchen for breakfast while you listen to him.

## *Comments*

If you are really cool, you can play *D*. But is it going to cost you some composure! You might think you can get the whole story from him, but how are you going to react if he confirms your worst fears? You might think you can go upstairs later to check out Frederick's story with your daughter's but what if they both concur or differ?

*A* is the reaction of a hysterical woman. You want to avoid extremes, so don't indulge in *A* even if your immediate reaction is to give vent to your emotions. This response is not going to endear you to Frederick who will look at you with a new disrespect for your lack of control. Screaming is not acceptable among Norwegians. Besides, he might have spent the night talking and playing chess with your daughter, then sleeping on cushions on the floor.

*C* is jumping to conclusions without giving either party a fair chance to explain. It is almost as bad as *A*. If you want to save face, don't involve Frederick's parents in the situation until you find out the true story. Norwegian parents tend to believe their own children are adult and responsible enough to account for their own actions. And there would be red faces all round if you have a meeting with Frederick's parents and nearly everyone in your household and then discover things were not what they seemed.

*B* seems to be the most reasonable solution. You are acting with dignity. Although you are dying of curiosity and feeling almost sick as you consider the possible intimacy between Frederick and your daughter, you want to give yourself time to react and to find out the truth from your daughter. And Frederick, who was on his way out anyway, gets to move on.

## *SITUATION 4*

You are a businessman who has come to Norway to win some contracts for your company. In your country or elsewhere, you have been actively involved in the persuasive power of incentives or small gestures – what others may call bribes – to clinch a winning deal. In Norway, you meet your contact for the first time and offer him an expensive gift. He declines politely and seems a bit flustered. You try to insist but you notice your client-to-be is uncomfortable about your gesture. What do you do?

*A* You realise that maybe this is not the tradition of conducting business deals in Norway and quickly change your tactics when you learn your cultural error. You withdraw the gift and lightly explain that in your country, it is normal to show respect to your hosts, especially those in a foreign country, by bringing gifts. You understand Norway does not have the same practice and you ask forgiveness for your faux pas.

B   You think your Norwegian contact is a smart cookie: he is angling for a bigger gift. You look at him askance and say aloud, 'Ah, I am sorry that my gift is so humble. I will send you another more appropriate gift when I get home. Tell me, what would you like?'

C   You can see that your gift will not be accepted and so you decide to change your strategy and offer another gift, an even bigger bribe. 'Have you been to my country? You haven't? Ah, you must come. Weather's lovely, the girls are beautiful, and the people are warm and friendly. You must come visit. In fact, I can arrange a trip for you soon after we negotiate this contract successfully. All expenses paid. And some pocket money for shopping as well. You'll see. It will be a good trip. You will like it. I guarantee that.'

D   You insist on his accepting the gift on behalf of his company. It is not your personal gift but a token from your company. And with these words of reassurance, you hope you have allayed his discomfort. You tell him the gift can be displayed in his office.

## Comments

As if the notion of accepting a gift is not complicated enough, you ask the poor man to display the gift in his office for all to see. *D* is definitely a no-no. How could you be so insensitive? You know that in Norway, the ethics of business communication is strongly upheld. To even seem to be breaching that code is tantamount to earning the distrust of the Norwegians who are already rather wary of you to begin with, simply because you come from a different country.

*C* is obviously going to make you popular with bribe-takers but not the ordinary Norwegian who is simple, upright, and honest. Your offer of a trip abroad smacks so clearly of bribery that you are insulting your Norwegian counterpart by even broaching this subject. The result might be that he is so wary of you and your modus operandi that he would not give your business proposal the consideration it might deserve.

*B* is as bad as *C*, only more subtle. You are indirectly conveying the message that you take your Norwegian counterpart's point. You understand that he wants a bigger bribe to grant you the deal.

You have misinterpreted the signs altogether, and if you had done your homework on the Norwegian business scene, you would know that Norwegians are almost immune to bribes. Moreover, they are so honest and sincere, almost naive, that they might not even understand the implications of your suggestion in *B*. Be careful how you tread. Norwegians go straight to the heart of the matter; there is little hedging and preamble about presents and gifts. What is your quotation? Where are your figures? These are what they want to know.

*A* is the most logical thing to do in the circumstances. You realise that in Norway they conduct business differently. And you are willing to go their way. You want to pave the way for effective business negotiation and you are quick-witted enough to explain away the gift as a cultural difference. On with the business!

## *SITUATION 5*

You are invited by your superior to spend a weekend with him and his family at their vacation chalet. You expect a weekend of luxury and splendour. Instead, you find yourself on a grassy mountain, sitting inside a small mountain cabin with only the basic amenities. There is electricity and hot water, but the toilet is outdoors in a makeshift shed and there is no flush system. The nearest homestead is on the next mountain. You are horrified by the primitiveness of it all. Your Norwegian host breathes in the fresh mountain air, looks at the mountains around, and smiles happily at you. He thinks you are as pleased as he is with his vacation home. What do you do?

*A* You smile back wanly, and mutter something like, 'How nice. What a surprise.' And then you take off to rummage in your rucksack for your tins of sardines and pack of cookies, wishing all the while you had had the foresight to bring more tins of food and changed your beautiful city shoes for jogging ones!

*B* You take a deep breath of the same mountain air and exclaim your surprise. You had not expected his summer home to be so simple and rustic, but what a lovely idea to go back to nature to commune and reflect and relax. You like it as much as he does. And you tell him so. Your surprise is genuine and sincere. And you want to learn to enjoy nature as your Norwegian associate does.

*C* You throw up your hands in despair, tear out tufts of your hair which fall to the ground to join the tufts of grass, and exclaim loudly, 'Well, you got me beat here, Olav! This was not what I expected. Not by a long shot. I thought we'd be eating caviar and dining on potatoes – yes, even potatoes again – and venison. And here we are – out in the open. I get claustrophobic in the open air, Olav. Thank you for bringing me here. Now when are we driving back home?'

*D* You are bewildered and upset. You had heard about vacation homes in Europe, and all the while you thought that only the well-to-do could afford them. This weekend in the mountains is not your idea of rest and recreation. You are just going to have to grin and bear it. And you do. But your face tells it all. You don't say anything negative or positive. You just smile and keep quiet.

## *Comments*

*D* will be most disturbing to your host who cannot fail to be affected by your lack of response to his enthusiasm. Pretty soon, he will guess you are not happy with the weekend he has planned for you, and his own enjoyment will be curtailed. You will not receive an invitation from him again. He has got your message, loud and clear.

*C* is outright rudeness and quite unforgivable if you remember that your Norwegian host is also your superior. Forget *C* and get on with your life. Nothing can be so bad. So what? There is grass and fresh air and mountain and water. Learn self-survival. Perhaps this is why your Norwegian boss invited you out to the mountain in the first place. It is a test of your capacity for adaptation and participation.

*A* is the mode of tolerance and deception. You could try it and still preserve the code of hospitality and status. But your lack of sincerity will soon be obvious unless you are a very good actor or learn to appreciate the simple pleasures of outdoor life.

*B* is the most sincere thing to say. Norwegians are honest and sincere, and they expect people they know to act likewise. It is a great honour to be invited to a Norwegian's vacation house if you remember just how much Norwegians treasure their privacy and personal or family time. So voice your appreciation, admit your surprise and be prepared to learn to understand the Norwegian in another context.

## SITUATION 6

You have recently settled into a Norwegian neighbourhood and are just getting to know your neighbours. Your child has a bicycle that he cycles around in the neighbourhood. One day, he returns home crying. On questioning him, you find that the five-year-old son of your neighbours two doors away has been throwing stones at him. You are concerned and go to the neighbours in question to inform them of their child's misdemeanour. The mother tells you quite coolly that it probably was an accident. You say you don't think it was – your child never lies. She replies that she will keep an eye on her son.

You soon find out that she is only giving lip service to her words because two days later, your son comes home with a swollen, bleeding lip and a bruised knee. The neighbours' son has been throwing stones at him again. This time, you are very angry and upset, and you go to your neighbour to complain. Again, the mother seems quite unperturbed and says she will check with her son. What do you do?

A You glare at your neighbour angrily and say that if she cannot control and discipline her son, then she needs help. And you stalk off, determined to make sure that the people in the neighbourhood know what an incorrigible child the young culprit is and what irresponsible neighbours the parents are.

B   You bring your child along with you to the neighbours' house and show the mother the bruises on his face and body. Then you tell her again that you are naturally quite upset. Her son is young but your son should not be subjected to hurt; you have told your son never to retaliate with physical violence although he might be bigger and he has obeyed. But enough is enough, and you expect some action to be taken to stop this irresponsible act of throwing stones.

C   You realise that you have so far been dealing with the mother, and now is the time for a new strategy. You tell your husband what has happened and ask him to pay a visit to the father of the young stone-thrower. You think the men will take this matter more seriously than the nonchalant mother who seems laconic and ill-willed towards you and your family.

D   You look at your neighbour with contempt on your face, and with a sneer you criticise her child-rearing skills. She must be a bad mother to have produced such a precocious bully. Before leaving, you tell her that you will make the matter a public issue (you're not quite sure how yet!) unless it is resolved immediately.

## Comments

D is liable to produce little result except anger on both sides. Your neighbour will react to your insult with strong emotions of dislike and perhaps try to account for your rude behaviour by saying that foreigners are so strange. But, seriously, never threaten Norwegians. They think those who make threats are impotent people who do not understand that Norwegians and their whole culture have never taken a threat as an impetus for action. On the contrary, it may produce the opposite result in that your neighbour will think you are unjustified in your criticism of her son because you are so unreasonable.

C might not be a bad idea though it is very likely that your neighbour has already mentioned the incident to her husband. Norwegians generally share child-rearing responsibilities jointly as couples and usually discuss their children and related problems together. So when you send your husband over to talk about the stone-throwing incident, you may be lessening their respect for your husband if he is perceived as being a measure of last resort. On the other hand, the culprit's father may be the stricter of the two parents and more concerned about how outsiders regard the family, and so he may act more quickly than the mother.

*B* seems to be the best solution. Seeing the injuries done to your child will convince the recalcitrant Norwegian mother that her son has been irresponsible. She has no reason to excuse him now, and so she will talk with him and perhaps keep him indoors as a punishment until he realises he cannot throw stones at people.

*A* is a hotheaded, insulting response that will get you nowhere. You have jumped to conclusions about your neighbour and made inappropriate comments. She certainly will be less inclined to heed your complaint as she can justify her lack of action by saying that you are a rude boor.

## SITUATION 7

You are a stay-at-home mother with two young children. You have been invited to lunch by your neighbour who is also looking after her children at home. This is your first invitation since your arrival and you are excited. You wonder what the meal will be like: meatballs with spaghetti, or perhaps a smørgåsbord? When you arrive at your hostess's house, you discover that lunch is only sandwiches! You are sorely disappointed because you had skipped breakfast in the expectation of a feast. What do you say and do?

A You exclaim with false exuberance, 'Ah, sandwiches! I love sandwiches! How nice.' And you try to control the hungry rumblings of your disappointed stomach and convince yourself that sandwiches can be quite exciting.

B You think what a bad hostess your new Norwegian friend is. Such cheapness – serving only sandwiches. Why, if you knew, you would have made your own and had them at home instead of walking all this way to eat them! But you try to swallow your disappointment and you say, 'Hmm ... Actually I had sandwiches for breakfast. I don't know if I can have them again for lunch.'

C You look as surprised as you feel and say, 'Oh, is this all you have for lunch? Why, in my country, we have a three-course meal for lunch. Lunch is really a solid affair. I must invite you to my house for lunch one day so you can see what it is like. And after that, you may never want to eat sandwiches for lunch again.'

D You say that it is a pleasant surprise to find that you are going to have sandwiches for lunch. In your culture, it is different. But you find that Norwegians seem to eat a lot of bread and this is a fascinating idea.

## *Comments*

*D* is a diplomatic and culturally engaging answer. You are being honest and sincere, and admitting that you had not expected sandwiches for lunch. Your hostess, who has invited you for the first time, is probably curious to find out more about your culture and this comment on sandwiches is a good starting point for an interesting conversation and an exchange of cultural differences and similarities. She will also appreciate your frankness, as most Norwegians do, and find it rather charming.

*C* is insulting and derogatory. You are putting down your hostess and her culture. As a result, you may never get invited to lunch again. So forget your disappointment and swallow your words if you want to be invited again – even if it is sandwiches.

*A* could be passed off, if performed adequately. But beware: Norwegians detest hypocrisy and falseness, and if they find you have been lying, they will not trust you again. Remember that Norwegians are a people of moderation and calmness. Excessive exuberance can jangle on their nerves and ring a warning bell. So do not overact the part of the enthusiastic sandwich-lover!

*B* is almost as bad as *C*. Your obviously caustic remarks will not go unnoticed. It is better to keep silent than to be rude. Your Norwegian hostess may take a while to figure out your rudeness, but she may be polite enough to ask if you would like something else for lunch. In which case, you can choose eggs, milk, waffles, or chocolate. Maybe.

## SITUATION 8

You are at home, playing custodian to the Norwegian neighbour's 10-year-old son, Anders, who is happily interacting with your own children. He is a gentle and considerate child and they are playing well together. You are all in the sitting room and suddenly, you hear a loud smacking noise against the glass window under the roof overlooking the sitting room.

You look up and realise that a bird has flown into the glass window above the sitting room. The children run out of the house to investigate. You are still in the sitting room when you look up just in time to see Anders climbing down from the roof. A couple of minutes later, the children are back in the sitting room and Anders is cradling the lifeless bird in his hands. He asks if he may bury it in the garden. Your own children are curious and concerned and seem quite keen to help him. What do you do?

*A* You look at Anders and launch into a tirade on how dangerous it was to have climbed onto the roof to get the bird. You accuse him of setting a bad example to your own children who will now feel inclined to climb up the roof at any time. You are upset and angry and forget his initial request, which is to bury the bird.

*B* You look at the little bird with sadness and say, 'Poor little thing! I should not have cleaned the windows last week. See, children, when your father next accuses me of not cleaning the windows, you know what to tell him. The windows become so clean that birds mistake the reflection for the real thing. So let's all learn not to clean windows – not for a long time again!'

*C* You look at the bird in Anders' hand and say, 'What a pity! It was a sad accident. Yes, you may bury the bird in the garden.' And then you address the children in general with a reminder that they should not feel they can climb up roofs anytime without asking your permission because they may hurt themselves. You do not do this to reprimand Anders but to remind the children of possible dangers when they climb roofs.

*D* You look at the dead bird and scream. You have never been near any dead bird at such close proximity, and you are shocked. You shriek and jump around, shouting, 'Take it away. Take it away. Bury it. Do anything with it. Throw it in the dustbin. But take it away from my sight. And wash your hands with soap afterwards!'

## Comments

*D* will not endear you to the children nor gain you respect. It is the unconditional response of a hysterical person who has never touched a bird nor seen death at close quarters. The children are naturally curious about nature and death. Your reaction may dissuade them from responding positively to the bird's death. They may follow your example and learn to be afraid of animals in nature. On the other hand, they may run off to bury the bird with Anders and then gossip about their scaredycat mother and be just a little scornful of your silliness.

*A* is an unwarranted attack on poor Anders. You become the authoritarian adult but you forget the issue at hand and focus only on what interests you, namely climbing up roofs. Children can only see the immediate issue, and your blurring of the incident can only earn their impatience and sympathy for Anders. Sometimes children see more clearly than adults riddled with worry. Meanwhile, Anders himself might be a little bewildered as to why you are blaming him for climbing up roofs. He has climbed trees and other heights, and his parents have allowed him to do so without castigation, emphasising only that he should know his own capabilities and practise caution where necessary. Norwegian children are confident in the outdoors. After all, it is their own backyard.

*B* is the response of a person who hates to wash windows. You have picked on the perfect excuse to get out of window-cleaning, but you are also unfairly implicating the children in a conflict that you obviously have with your spouse.

*C* is the most reasonable and adult answer you can give. It is rational and logical. You answer Anders' query as to whether he can bury the bird. At the same time, you also show you are concerned with example-setting and climbing up roofs.

## *SITUATION 9*

The organisation where you work impresses you with its staff work ethic and individual initiative. The staff are hardworking and prompt with their work. They show creativity and interest and spend time to discuss issues when necessary. But you still cannot adjust to the concept of working time in Norway. One day, a crisis pops up and you expect the staff to stay overtime to thresh it out. You are at an important juncture in a meeting. It is nearly 4 o'clock and you can see some staff looking at their watches and fidgeting in their chairs. You know they are impatient to go home, but it is important to you that the issue be resolved once and for all. What do you do?

A You look at the restless staff and say admonishingly, 'Lars, stop fidgeting in your chair – you're making me nervous. And Stein, you can stop glancing at your watch. I know what the time is as well as you do. We've got a problem on our hands and we've got to resolve it today before we go home. So let's order some sand-wiches. You can call home to say you are not going back for dinner yet. I expect we shall be finished in another two hours. So stay put. We've got work to do!'

B You look around at the discussion table enquiringly and ask everyone, 'Look. I know it is coming to 4 o'clock. It is time for us to go home. But we have got a crisis on our hands. I would suggest that we stay on to discuss the problem and come up with a resolution. What do you say? Another option is to break off for dinner and come back to the office two hours from now. Tell me your ideas. I'd appreciate it. But I really think coming up with an appropriate resolution of this problem is imperative.' And then you leave it to the staff to generate their comments.

C You look at your watch and you say, 'Ah! It's coming to 4 o'clock. My goodness! How the time flies. Where have we come to with our

WE SEEM TO HAVE A SUDDEN CRISIS...

problem? Not far, I think. We need to stay on and brainstorm some more. I wish Norwegians wouldn't keep an eye on the time. Work is important, you know. Why can't you all work till 5 p.m. like in other countries? What can we do if we all break off at 4 p.m. every day? When I arrived in Norway, I thought the working times were ridiculous. I have now been in Norway for seven months, and I still think the working hours are ridiculous. Can you enlighten me as to why Norwegians work such short hours?' And you look around for a Norwegian philosopher at the table.

D  You begin to get annoyed at the obvious signs of restlessness and get all self-righteous. 'That's right. Look at your watches. Think of the warm dinner waiting for you at home. You have all got homes to go back to. So have I. But the difference between you and me is that I care about the company. I care about my work. And if my work isn't completed on time, I'll stay back to do it. Look here. Today, I'll be staying back again. Who will stay back with me? I'll bet none of you will. We are at a critical point in our negotiations and all you can think about is 4 o'clock and your stomachs and families. It's so unfair. I could go home too but I won't. Norwegians just don't care. Your work ethic is terrible. All you want is your free time. The company comes second …'

## *Comments*

*D* is the worst thing to do as you alienate the staff and emphasise your foreignness all the more. You insult the Norwegians in general and you imply that you are the only one who cares about the company, which is of course not true. Your action is unreasonable and your staff will not show you support thereafter when they see your accusatory stance and belligerent attitude. You might win your bet.

*C* is not advisable as you are going off on another tangent in your query for clarification of a national routine. The last thing you want in a crisis is a distraction. If you adopt *C*, you are showing weaknesses as an effective leader and group manager because you are leading everyone off the track and wasting time. You are also criticising a Norwegian institution – the concept of working hours. This will make Norwegians defensive and irritated. They can see that you are in a bad humour and are resentful. And they will just up and leave when 4 o'clock comes because they perceive the uselessness of the ensuing conversation – if it takes off.

*A*, the authoritarian approach, may do quite well in other countries where it will be perceived as exercising leadership prowess and authority. However, in Norway, people do not like to be talked down to. You will not produce any cooperative gestures from your staff, and if they do stay on, they will do so with reluctance and resentment. It is more likely, though, that someone in the room will raise an objection to your high-handedness. You have not bothered to find out what they want. You have just been dictatorial and given your orders, and they are not happy. What can you do if half the people in the room walk off at 4 p.m. and the others stay on halfheartedly? Would you have been effective in your communication?

*B* is the best course of action because it gives room for manoeuvre and exchange of views. It allows the staff to give you their recommendations and at the same time draws renewed respect from them because you acknowledge their significance in the decision-making process. The consultative approach works well in Norway where consensus and teamwork are important for group cooperation and corporate strategy. In all likelihood, the staff would agree with you that there is a crisis and it is vital it be settled before the end of the day. And they volunteer to stay back to resolve the issue. You have a cooperative pool of people who will tackle the issue with energetic resourcefulness because they are concerned and they also want to get back home before midnight.

Norwegians do work overtime but they would prefer to be told in advance. You should not tell them one hour before 4 p.m. Tell them a day in advance, if you can, so that they can adjust their personal schedules.

## *SITUATION 10*

You are new in the neighbourhood and are lucky enough to find a neighbourhood kindergarten for your toddler. You are excited and happy when you bring your child to the kindergarten for the first day. You stay around for a little while and see the kids running around in the garden compound under adult supervision, some even climbing trees. The kindergarten has its own routine and timetable and you find that your child is going to spend a lot of time outdoors. It begins to snow lightly. The kids are all dressed in appropriate winter jackets and boots and are playing happily in the garden still. You are horrified. This is the first winter for you and your family in Norway. And you have always associated winter with huddling indoors, in warm clothes, drinking hot cocoa and keeping warm. This idea of playing in snowy weather bewilders you. What do you do?

*A* You see the kindergarten principal and voice your disquiet vociferously. Your eloquence impresses her but not in the way you expected. She explains that children in Norway are taught to respect nature and live with it, and outdoor play is an expression of this respect and learning. You disagree vehemently and vow to take your child out of the kindergarten with immediate effect if all she is going to do is play in the snow where she will catch her death of cold. How could the teachers be so irresponsible? Are they so lazy as to want the children to run around most of the time and not learn anything much in the classroom? You stalk off to make sure your child is not playing in the dangerous snow.

*B* You look with wonder at this winter-play and encourage your child to join her new classmates. You are a little worried that she might catch cold in the snow but if the Norwegian children can take it, so can your child.

*C* You ask a teacher what the meaning of all this outdoor activity is. You thought that a kindergarten should teach basic knowledge skills like the alphabet and counting. There should be a time for play but mainly indoor play, you thought. You explain that your child is prone to colds and asthma and you hope the teachers in charge will take adequate care to protect her. You want her to join in the play but you don't want her to get sick.

D  You look at the snow, at the children in the snow, and at your little girl looking with glee at the children in the snow. You are in a quandary. You decide she shouldn't play in the snow this first day. You explain your caution. 'You might catch cold, dear. And you mustn't climb the trees, you know. You might hurt yourself. Don't follow those Norwegian children. They have been here longer than we have. We'd better wait first and see how it really is. Listen to mummy, okay? I want you to be safe. And it is not safe to climb trees and play in the snow.'

## *Comments*

D is the response of a wet blanket and an over-cautious parent. You want to adapt to your new environment and are understandably wary about the different ways of doing things. But to kill your child's eagerness and excitement is most damaging. You want to stimulate her interest and curiosity, and D is absolutely the wrong way to go about doing it. Your child might respond in two ways: heed your advice and thereafter be very cautious in her interaction with Norwegian children; or just ignore you and play with the other children because she is spontaneous and eager to learn and experience new things like winter snow.

C is a perfectly logical response from a concerned parent with a child who is not exactly sickly but is susceptible to colds and weather conditions. It is an admission of caution and a request for consideration from the teachers in charge. Norwegian teachers will respect your request, but will also probably tell you that snow does not necessarily cause colds. It might be good for your child to have fresh, crisp winter air, especially if she is prone to asthma, which is related to atmospheric impurities.

*A* is a typical paranoid parent's response. You are insisting on being ethnocentric in your perception and understanding of Norwegian culture and outdoor life. And you do not want to see that the outdoors and nature play an important role in any Norwegian child's learning process. When you threaten to take your child out of the kindergarten, know that the Norwegian principal takes your threat seriously. If you attempt to put your child back in the same kindergarten a few days later, you will be told in no uncertain terms that her place has been given to someone else on the waiting list. Yes. There is a waiting list of children for kindergarten. You were very fortunate to have got a place for your child, but you did not appreciate your good fortune. And now you have to hunt for another kindergarten in the vicinity, which will not be an easy thing to do. Even if you finally find a kindergarten for your child, you will discover that all Norwegian kindergartens have outdoor play as a significant part of their programme. It is part of the national agenda for pre-primary education.

*B* is a wonderful, free and easy response that will show the Norwegians how adaptable you are. In this reaction, you are truly trying to adapt to your new and strange situation with great aplomb. You are adventurous and eager to learn, and your child will be infused with the same energy and enthusiasm. Together, you will adapt beautifully in Norway.

# BIBLIOGRAPHY

The following list provides a varied reading range for those interested in finding out more about the various aspects of life and culture in Norway. In no way is the list comprehensive; it merely represents a selection of materials to stimulate and hopefully satisfy, to a reasonable degree, the curiosity of readers. If you want to learn more about the literature of Norway, you should refer to English translations of literary works, such as the plays of Henrik Ibsen. This bibliography is limited to texts available in the English language.

If you are inspired to learn the Norwegian language, you could pick up the language skills through courses and coursebooks. I would recommend Hugo's *Learn Norwegian in 3 Months*, which I used with the aid of a native speaker to provide pronunciation guidance along the way.

## *INTRODUCTION TO NORWAY*

**John Midgård, *A Brief History of Norway*, Oslo: Johan Grundt Tanum Forlag, 1963, 1971.**
This book is a sufficiently concise introduction to the history of Norway, spanning the years from the Viking Age and Saga Age through turbulent times to modern Norway in the early 1970s. It presents an overview that is at once informed and enlightening. The section on the early kings of Norway gives a fascinating account of how Norwegian history is dotted with legacies of Harald Fairhair who first united Norway before A.D. 900, Erik Bloodaxe, Håkon the Good, Harald Graypelt (so named because of his style of dress), Olav the Peaceful (Olav III), Magnus Sigurdson the Blind, and Magnus Håkonson the Lawmender. Midgård also gives a list of Norwegian

political leaders from 1814 to 1971, and this is interesting because of the light it casts on the influence of the political parties in the country.

If you want to go on to further reading and catch up with the times, you should read the next book on the list.

**Ivar Libaek and Øivind Stenerson,** *History of Norway: From the Ice Age to the Oil Age,* **trans. Joan Fuglesang and Virginia Singer, Oslo: Grøndahl og Dreyers Forlag AS, 1991, 1992.**
This is a highly readable account of Norway's development. It is a widely read book, having been translated into English, German, French, and Spanish. There are 19 theme sections on issues such as emigration, Norwegian shipping, the Sami people, Norsk Hydro (the main supplier of hydroelectric energy in Norway), and Norway as an oil nation. The combination of text, illustrations, maps, and diagrams gives the subjects discussed depth and inclusiveness.

The book presents Norwegian history from the earliest times to the present day, and describes Norway's international ties and involvement through the ages. It introduces great personalities like St. Olav, the king who tried to Christianise Norway and was killed at Sticklestad and canonised shortly thereafter, and Christian Frederick, the king who witnessed the making of the Constitution of independent Norway in 1814. The book also examines the impact of Norway's oil on the lifestyle and politics of the country. The presentation is lucid and coherent, with a good overview of important issues.

## CHILDREN'S LITERATURE

**Asbjørnsen and Moe,** *A Time for Trolls: Fairy Tales from Norway,* **trans. Joan Roll-Hansen, Oslo: Nor-Media AS, 1962, 1986.**
Asbjørnsen and Moe are credited with being the chroniclers of Norwegian folktales. These two men travelled around Norway, collecting all kinds of tales and recording stories which would otherwise have been lost through the uncertain continuity of the oral

tradition. Like their Danish counterpart, Hans Christian Andersen, Asbjørnsen and Moe accumulated a wealth of literature, which has been handed down through the generations to the present day.

This little collection relates the exploits of Askeladden – a Norwegian Aladdin – who is the male version of Cinderella, sitting by the ashes, laughed at by his two elder brothers till he goes out into the world and proves himself. In tales that will enchant and charm children and adults, Askeladden shows that a willingness to commune with the world and nature can lead to the discovery of hidden powers. Combined with his natural traits and strengths such as steadfastness and great wit, Askeladden conquers the trolls, the creatures of Norwegian darkness (distinguished by their tails, which they try desperately to hide), and his readers the world over.

## FOOD

**Kjell E. Innli, *The Norwegian Kitchen* (recipes provided by the Association of Norwegian Chefs), Kristiansund: KOM Forlag AS, 1993.**

This beautifully illustrated book is a comprehensive introduction to the Norwegian kitchen and popular Norwegian recipes. It is divided into two sections. The first part describes the kitchen in depth, examining the role of climate and crops in the Norwegian culinary heritage. The historical perspective contrasts coastal with inland cultures and provides an illuminating insight into the production process and the context that gave rise to the typical Norwegian diet.

The Chefs' Guild in each county in Norway collected recipes, and the second part of the book presents 350 selected recipes on soups, porridge, fish, game, and other dishes – a very rich representation of food from the Norwegian kitchen. A little drawback is the unwieldy size of the book, but this does not deter it from being a lovely and useful addition to your kitchen library.

# BUSINESS

**Brian Goth, *In the Desert of the Blue-Eyed Arabs: Cross-Cultural Management in the Norwegian Oil Industry from an Expatriate Perspective*, Working Paper 85/12, Oslo: Bedriftsokonomisk Institutt, Norwegian School of Management, 1985.**

Brian Goth is an Australian professor who has resided for many years in Norway. His 1985 working paper gives a crisp summation of the principal features of Norwegian businessmen in the oil industry, viewpoints that are culled from detailed questionnaires answered by 64 managers from four multinational oil companies. Eleven nationalities were represented, with the overwhelming majority belonging to five national groups – American, French, British, Canadian, and Dutch. Almost all the respondents worked in the Stavanger area in southwest Norway.

In this analytical and objective study, Goth comes up with some interesting pronouncements about the Norwegian business personality, traits that still hold true today. Drawing on historical and sociological perspectives, he imparts a perceptive understanding of the cultural complexity of the Norwegian character.

**Price Waterhouse, *Doing Business in Norway (Information Guide)*, USA: Price Waterhouse World Firm Limited, 1960, 1988.**

This is a wonderfully practical guidebook for those who want to do business in Norway. It discusses the laws and regulations pertaining to trading, employment, and investment, and describes the investment climate in Norway. In its profile of Norway, the book looks at the economy, population, and social patterns and throws in some hints for visiting business people. It also explores business options and entities in Norway and checks out issues like public and private sector cooperation, labour management relations, implications of Norway's membership in the European Community, and overseas trade relations. The book ends with an explanation of audit and accounting practices in Norway, and taxation law relating to companies and individuals. This is a handy guide to corporate culture in Norway.

## CULTURE

**Vera Henriksen, *Christmas in Norway: Past and Present*, Oslo: Tanum-Norli, 1970, 1981.**
To people in many parts of the world, Christmas is associated with snow and ice. And Santa Claus with his reindeer, the symbol of the season, supposedly dwells at the North Pole. Somehow, perhaps because of its winter climate and proximity to the North Pole, Norway has gained the reputation of being a Christmas country. A byproduct of this Christmas lore is that every year at Christmas time, a number of letters addressed to Santa Claus in Norway arrive in the country.

This book provides a glimpse into the celebration of Christmas in Norway and shows how the various strands of tradition, new and ancient, pagan and Christian, are interwoven to form a rich tapestry of customs and rituals. You can read about the *jule øl* or Christmas beer, drunk in medieval times from an elegant drinking horn; the Yule candle that kept the light burning through Christmas Eve, the *julenisse* or Christmas elf, and straw men and straw magic, a custom inherited from the harvest rite.

**Patricia Crinton Bjåland, *Living in Norway: A Practical Guide*, Oslo: P.C. Bjåland, 1985.**
The book gives very practical information for foreigners who are settling down in Norway. It gives day to day details which are presented in a very readable way. Although published in the mid-1980s, it is still a very useful book. But note that parts of the legislation referred to have been amended; likewise the prices on services are no longer applicable.

# ACKNOWLEDGEMENTS

I acknowledge, with gratitude, the assistance and support of the following people and corporations:

Kvaerner Singapore Pte Ltd
Kvaerner Fjellstrand (S) Pte Ltd
Den Norske Bank AS
Christian Norberg-Schulz
Ingrid Espelid-Høvig
Eva Mølsæter
Eric Cameron
Cornelia Horn
Tom and Bodil Bergan
Paul Su

I would also like to thank the many other individuals, too numerous to mention, who gave unstintingly of their time to discussions on Norwegian culture and lifestyle. Without the support and encouragement of my husband Ole, *Culture Shock! Norway* would not have been possible.

# THE AUTHOR

Elizabeth Su-Dale and her Norwegian husband, Ole Johan, an architect and urban planner, have lived in Norway for four years at a stretch. When they went to Norway, they had three children. They left Norway with four children in tow.

Elizabeth has worked variously as a university lecturer in English, a research officer at the National Museum in Singapore, and a scriptwriter-presenter with Radio Singapore. Her museum stint awakened her interest in history and culture and she continued to nurture this curiosity in things cultural when she worked on her 40-segment series on Singapore culture for Radio Singapore in 1987. A follow-up to this is her more recent project with NTUC – National Trades Union Congress – Radio in 1993.

*Culture Shock! Norway* is the natural outgrowth of her spontaneous delight in the vibrancy and tradition of Norwegian culture and her desire to share her experience with others. In Norway, Elizabeth was a member of the Women's Study Group, a more professionally-oriented informal contact group for working women, and an active Study Leader in the Housewives' Group, a large and popular organisation for all women residing in Norway. The latter organisation is devoted to the support of family and women's rights and roles and is represented in the Norwegian Parliament. To promote cultural exchange, Elizabeth organised enjoyable culinary exchanges among the different cultures in her district. Because of her children, she also found herself recruited into the Scout movement in Norway.

Presently, Elizabeth and her family are living in Singapore where they are trying to rediscover the joys of bicycling and baking bread in an Asian urban context.

# INDEX